This book is about the spiritual power
that you can bring into
bar and bat mitzvah

This book was read by

_____

Name of parents, grandparents, child, relatives, friend

To prepare for the bar/bat mitzvah ceremony of

_____

Child's name

_____

Date

_____

Torah portion

_____

Name of synagogue and community

This book was a gift from

_____

Putting God on the Guest List

How to Reclaim the Spiritual Meaning of Your Child's Bar or Bat Mitzvah

~~~~

Rabbi Jeffrey K. Salkin

Foreword by Rabbi Sandy Eisenberg Sasso
Introduction by Rabbi William H. Lebeau

JEWISH LIGHTS Publishing
Woodstock, Vermont

Library of Congress Cataloging-in-Publication Data

Salkin, Jeffrey K., 1954–
    Putting God on the guest list: how to reclaim the spiritual meaning of your child's bar or bat mitzvah / Jeffrey K. Salkin

Includes bibliographical references (p. 176)
    1. Bar mitzvah—Handbooks, manuals, etc. 2. Bat mitzvah—Handbooks, manuals, etc. 3. Jewish way of life—Handbooks, manuals, etc. 4. Jewish youth—Religious life—Handbooks, manuals, etc. 5. Commandments (Judaism)—Handbooks, manuals, etc. I. Title

BM707.2.S25 1992
296.4'424—dc20

92-6404
CIP

ISBN 1-879045-20-6 (cloth)
ISBN 1-879045-10-9 (paper)

First edition
10 9 8 7 6 5 4 3 2 1

Manufactured in the United States of America

Published by JEWISH LIGHTS Publishing
A Division of LongHill Partners, Inc.
P.O. Box 237
Sunset Farm Offices, Route 4
Woodstock, Vermont 05091
Tel: (802) 457-4000
Fax: (802) 457-4004

"In The Synagogue" by Cynthia Ozick is reprinted by permission of the author and her agents, Raines & Raines, 71 Park Avenue, New York, NY 10016.

To my mother, Sidonia Karpel Salkin, of blessed memory,
who taught me to love words and wisdom.

To Nina and Samuel,
who taught me to magically transform a home into an altar.

Contents

Putting God on the Guest List is written for:

- Parents of young people who are about to become bar or bat mitzvah, who are looking for inspiration and meaning in their upcoming *simchah.*

- Grandparents of young people who are about to become bar or bat mitzvah, who are looking to reclaim that sense of holy purpose and may want to reacquaint themselves with the customs and meanings of these sacred moments.

- A young man or woman who is preparing to become bar or bat mitzvah, who wants to find some deeper meaning beyond learning Torah and *haftarah.*

- An adult who is becoming an adult bar or bat mitzvah—to see how these meanings might become reflected in his or her own life.

- Professionals and lay leaders in the Jewish community—rabbis, cantors, educators, tutors, and synagogue leaders—who would like to reinvigorate bar/bat mitzvah within their own synagogues.

- Non-Jewish friends and family members, who will be attending a bar or bat mitzvah ceremony and want to understand its deeper historical and theological meaning.

- Christian clergy, who may want to use *Putting God on the Guest List* as a model for the spiritual "upgrading" of confirmation.

Acknowledgments

Putting God on the Guest List represents the culmination of more than a decade of thought and struggle with the American Jewish institution of bar and bat mitzvah.

Putting God on the Guest List could not have come to light without the guidance, help, and support of many people. First, my teacher and colleague, Rabbi Lawrence Hoffman, professor of liturgy at Hebrew Union College-Jewish Institute of Religion. Professor Hoffman challenged me to think anew about liturgy, worship, and ritual. He introduced me to the possibility of looking at rituals and texts not only through eyes trained by the Jewish tradition, but through eyes that also understood psychology, anthropology, and sociology. Without his mentoring, I would never have thought of looking at bar and bat mitzvah in the way that I have chosen. He has shown me the stars. For this, I am eternally grateful.

To my teachers at Princeton Theological Seminary. *Putting God on the Guest List* emerged out of thought processes that began while doing my doctoral work on bar and bat mitzvah ritual. Professor Tom Long was my dissertation advisor at Princeton. From the moment we first "met" over the phone there was a blessed rapport. Turning my doctoral work into *Putting God on the Guest List* was initially his idea.

To my congregation, Central Synagogue of Nassau County, in Rockville Centre, New York. Central Synagogue was the true laboratory for my work on bar and bat mitzvah, and my congregants have encouraged the process by which I have begun to transform the liturgical expression of bar and bat mitzvah. Many stories and comments in this book have come out of my experience at Central Synagogue and in my two former congregations, Temple Judea of Bucks County, Doylestown, Pennsylvania, and Temple Israel of Greater Miami, Florida. Robert Wurwarg and Linda Levine, loyal congregants and parents of a soon-to-be bat mitzvah, read earlier versions of this manuscript. Their suggestions have been extremely valuable. Joel Hoffman of Excelsior Computer Services, Silver Spring, Maryland, made both the Hebrew texts and his copyrighted translations of many of the prayers available.

To my publisher, Stuart Matlins of Jewish Lights Publishing. He and his associate, Jevin Eagle, have been beacons of light—guiding and sustaining this project, adding innumerable comments and suggestions, always thinking creatively and lovingly. I have grown immeasurably as a writer through my partnership with them. I thank God for our friendship. The words of this book were sculpted and shaped, fretted over and reworked, joyfully stroked and playfully poked, by my editor *extraordinaire,* Arthur Magida. His efforts were above and beyond the call of duty. My secretary, Minnie Brody, put up with numerous pressures throughout the creation of this manuscript, handling all of them with her characteristic grace and making my life easier in the process. In addition, thanks also to Rabbi Eric Lankin of West Hempstead, New York, Rabbi William Lebeau of the Jewish Theological Seminary of America, and Rabbi Sandy Sasso of Indianapolis, Indiana, who read early drafts and made some invaluable suggestions on content and style.

To my wife Nina Rubin Salkin and our son Samuel Asher Salkin. Nina has been incredibly nurturing. When my spirits darkened, she urged me to continue, though she surely knew that my many hours of work would absent me from the family. I can now turn such time over to my family where it rightfully belongs. My achievement is their achievement as well.

Finally, to the One God Who sustains us and teaches us, and to Whom our prayers must ultimately turn. You have blessed me with strength and with purpose. To You, Eternal One, I am grateful.

Jeffrey K. Salkin
Rockville Centre, NY
April, 1992

Foreword

Most of bar and bat mitzvah preparation focuses on synagogue skills, Hebrew language, and chanting, while most parents of *benei mitzvah* focus on party planning, invitations, and guest lists. Adults worry about whether they can afford their friends, and youngsters worry whether they can get through the Torah reading without a glaring error.

Intellectual challenge and skill acquisition are important. Uncertain that they can accomplish anything well in the adult world, as they move through the ever-changing, ambivalent time of puberty, *benei mitzvah* take great personal pride in displaying Hebrew competence and liturgical leadership. Celebration among family and friends is not a luxury. In a world of increasing fragmentation and mobility, the need for moments of binding is critical to communal connectedness.

And yet, bar and bat mitzvah is more than simply a graduation, an affirmation of intellect, and an excuse for a party. It is the confirmation of character development, a window to the sacred. We need ever more opportunities to help our children learn the difference between being smart and being wise. As they begin to put on deodorant, as their voices change and they menstruate or have wet dreams for the first time, it is not enough to teach our children how to make a blessing. We must also teach them how to *be* a blessing. They need to know God, not just from the prayerbook, but from life, to see God in acts of kindness and in pursuit of peace. As their teachers and parents, we want them to bring God into the world by being fair, honorable, considerate. As they develop physically and mentally, we need to help them develop spiritually and to exercise their soul.

Bar and bat mitzvah is too often a time for unwrapping presents when it should be a time for unwrapping the gifts of the spirit that created the art and literature, the heroic deeds and moral teachings of our people.

I have worked with *benei mitzvah* for many years. They worry about whether they are too tall for thirteen or too short to see over the pulpit. We should encourage them to measure themselves by the breadth of their wisdom and the expanse of their heart.

While the bar mitzvah has for centuries been a rite of passage for men, the opportunity for young women to become *benot mitzvah,* which began in 1922, has not only enriched women's personal lives but Jewish communal life as well. Studies in adolescence find that girls emerge from their teenage years with a poor self-image and much less confidence in their abilities than boys. Bat mitzvah is a door to self-esteem. It says that girls count, that their voice and experience are integral parts of a sacred community. As adolescent girls and increasing numbers of adult women ascend the *bimah* to become *benot mitzvah,* they are building a home and a memory for future generations.

I write these words just months before my own daughter becomes a bat mitzvah. I hope to tell her: "There was a time when women were told what they could *not* be. Then there came a time when women were told what they *needed* to be, if they wanted success. But I want you to know: There is nothing as a woman you cannot be, and there are two things you need to be—true to yourself and responsible to your community."

> WHAT I WISH FOR MY DAUGHTER,
> I WISH FOR ALL OUR CHILDREN.
> I wish for you to be a
> person of character
> strong but not tough,
> gentle but not weak.
>
> I wish for you to be
> righteous but not self-righteous
> honest but not unforgiving.
>
> Wherever you journey, may your steps be firm
> and may you walk in just paths
> and not be afraid.

Whenever you speak, may your words
be words of wisdom and friendship.

May your hands build
and your heart preserve what is good
and beautiful in our world.

May the voices of the generations of our people
move through you
and may the God of our ancestors
be your God as well.

May you know that there is a people,
a rich heritage, to which you belong
and from that sacred place
you are connected to all who dwell on the earth.

May the stories of our people
be upon your heart
and the grace of the Torah rhythm
dance in your soul.

Putting God on the Guest List is Rabbi Jeffrey Salkin's invitation to all families, to link the sacred act of "going up" to the Torah with the sacred process of "growing up" in faithfulness to God and community.

Rabbi Sandy Eisenberg Sasso
Beth-El Zedeck Congregation
Indianapolis, Indiana

Introduction

In this valuable book, Rabbi Jeffrey Salkin urgently invites parents, children becoming bar or bat mitzvah, and the entire Jewish community to recapture the spiritual meaning of one of the most critical moments for determining a Jewish child's connection to our tradition and to God.

Each family approaches the guest list for its bar or bat mitzvah with care, for it is clear that the nature of the event will be influenced by those who attend. We carefully plan accommodations for our guests. With sensitivity we tend to travel arrangements and special dietary requirements. And yet, the most important element of all may be taken for granted or neglected. Have we remembered to extend an invitation to God? Have we planned the bar and bat mitzvah in a way that God's comfort and dignity will be assured throughout our services and celebration?

Despite tales of crass bar or bat mitzvah celebrations, I have found that most often the religious and social celebrations of this moment of transition in Jewish life have succeeded in bringing the young man or woman into serious contact with God, perhaps for the first time. As a congregational rabbi, I enjoyed the privilege of standing on the bimah as more than eleven hundred thirteen-year-olds were called to the Torah to consider their connection to God, the Torah, and the Jewish people. I also taught many of these young people in our community's Hebrew High School programs. Four years after their bar or bat mitzvah, I would ask them to write a statement describing the times in their lives when they felt closest to God. So many responded to my question with powerfully affirming statements about their bar or bat mitzvah. They decribed how reading from the Torah, chanting and standing before the Ark on that day created a moment with God that continued to touch them.

The feelings of these young men and women were also recounted by many older adults whom I encountered when they came to my synagogue seeking a fuller Jewish identity. In discussing what had sustained their connection to Judaism, they said they had never forgotten the feelings of comfort and closeness with God they had experienced on that special day of youthful spirituality.

I believe that we, as parents and educators, can learn to deepen the meaning of bar and bat mitzvah for our children and our families. We can capture the spiritual, religious awakenings set in the ritual of our tradition and enhanced by the sacred setting of the sanctuary. Rabbi Salkin's book takes this challenge seriously. He offers us a wise and insightful presentation that suggests how the young Jewish child becoming a man or woman can encounter God in transition from dependence to emerging adulthood. Rabbi Salkin also explains why the tears we cry when a bar or bat mitzvah reaches out to touch the Torah for the first time, not only reflect our joy, but also measure our anxiety. We rejoice in our realization that the years of Jewish continuity in our family will not end with us. But we worry about the influences in today's Jewish life that threaten the link just formed between past and future generations by the young Jew standing before us.

The author speaks with candor, yet offers encouragement to the many children and their parents who face the difficulties of the changing Jewish family. The tensions of divorce and remarriage, intermarriage, conversion, and grandparents of different faiths jeopardize the pursuit of spirituality at a bar or bat mitzvah. The full and open discussion of these issues in *Putting God on the Guest List,* however, gives us hope that even these concerns can be addressed. God can be invited and afforded a place of dignity, even in the midst of crisis. God's Presence can help the child transcend his or her adversity with a new measure of comfort and confidence.

Perhaps the most intense tears at a bar or bat mitzvah are shed for the simultaneous joy and anxiety that are kindled when we contemplate the issue of freedom. We celebrate the child's newly acquired adult privilege of freedom to choose. We rejoice for the freedom granted Jews in today's society. Yet how fearful we are, for the freedoms are so vast and the society so accepting.

It is a dilemma, not unlike the moment in the Garden of Eden when God watches with anxiety as Adam and Eve reach out to take the fruit of the forbidden tree of the knowledge of good and evil. The narrative describes God's ambivalence about these first "children" becoming something more than children. God points out the tree of knowledge of good and evil and urges Adam and Eve to protect their childlike innocence by not exercising their freedom to choose. "And the Lord God commanded . . . 'Of every tree of the garden you may freely eat; but of the tree of the knowledge of good and evil you shall not eat of it; for in the day you eat thereof you [your innocence] shall surely die.'" The Wisdom of God anticipates the anguish Adam and Eve, and their descendants, will encounter once they discover their power to freely choose and influence their own destiny.

Still, the act of eating from the tree should not be viewed as the failure of the occupants of Eden. When they reach out to the tree, God does not prevent them from eating. The story's most important lesson is that God will not stand in our way, for only by exercising choice can we become fully human, with the potential to reflect the image of God in which we were created. That is why God comments after Adam and Eve have eaten, "Behold, the man and woman have become as one of us [like God] to know good and evil. . . ."

The story of the Garden of Eden has yet another dimension. There is a second tree planted in the midst of the garden called the *Eitz Hachayim*—the tree of life. It was not forbidden to Adam and Eve. They had the opportunity to taste of that tree as well and "eat and live forever," or at least learn from this tree how to contribute to the world in a way that their presence on earth would have everlasting value. The tree of life would have provided a balance for their newly acquired knowledge of good and evil. God would have welcomed their eating its fruit. Regrettably, they did not choose to taste it.

Today at the moment of bar and bat mitzvah the young Jew is offered a similar lesson. He or she is called before the Torah, which in Jewish tradition is also called *Eitz Chayim*. The reader points to a word and in effect offers the young person the opportunity to taste of the tree of life. The critical moment comes when the child decides to touch the Torah. The words of the Torah are brought, symbolically, to his or her mouth to be devoured as food for thought and instruction. Finally the bar or bat mitzvah grasps the Torah itself as a sign of recognition that this tree—God's Tree of Life—offers the source of guidance for a full, productive, moral life.

Rabbi Salkin stimulates us to imagine the full possibilities for the next bar and bat mitzvah, in our personal families or in the larger family of the Jewish community. He makes it clear that without God's Presence, this moment in Jewish life will lose its promise.

A distinguished Reform rabbi, Rabbi Salkin once again demonstrates how vital it is for Jews of every segment of our community to share ideas. His book offers guidance to all Jews, no matter what their affiliation. His religious passion and concern for the future of the Jewish people is evident in every chapter. Above all his love for God, and his confidence that God and religious experience can be found in Jewish rituals and celebration like bar and bat mitzvah, will inspire the Jewish community to treasure this sacred experience even more.

Rabbi William H. Lebeau, *Vice-chancellor*
Jewish Theological Seminary of America

Why This Book Was Born

Moses ascends Mount Sinai to receive the tablets of the covenant. "Adonai said to Moses, 'Come up to me on the mountain *veyeheh sham,* and *be there.*'" (Exodus 24:12)

Menachem Mendl of Kotsk, a great Chasidic teacher, asked, "If Moses had come up the mountain, why did God also have to tell him to *'be there'?*" Because, the Chasid answered, it is possible to expend great effort in climbing a mountain, but still not *be there*. Not everyone who is there is *there*. Sometimes they're somewhere else.

Bar and bat mitzvah is a sacred mountain in Jewish time. We climb this particular mountain because it brings us closer to God, closer to Judaism, closer to our people, closer to ourselves. And what modern Jews need, more than ever, is a way to really *be* there at the summit of this holy mountain.

You started walking a Jewish path decades ago. Now your children are starting to walk the same path. It is a path up a sacred mountain, a mountain very similar to Sinai, yet very much our own. Parents want to appreciate the full richness of the bar and bat mitzvah experience; they want their children to also experience it fully. They know that bar and bat mitzvah marks the passage from Jewish childhood to the beginnings of Jewish maturity. They seek Jewish tools that will help them and their child make that sacred journey.

Bar and bat mitzvah are among the most popular American Jewish rituals. Yet, few understand their history and deeper theological implications. They are more than a glitzy theme party, more than a moment of ethnic nostalgia. They are a glorious moment in the life of the family, the synagogue, and the Jewish people. And yet, over the years bar and bat mitzvah have too often become a banal event, a confused event, a ridiculed event, an event that sometimes lacks meaning because we are not sure what it *should* mean, because we have not learned how to *be* at the mountain.

Traditionally, bar and bat mitzvah occurred as part of the natural rhythm of a family's life. This is still true for committed, involved

Jewish families. By "committed" and "involved," which I am using in a nondenominational way, I mean those Jews who care about Judaism, who seek Jewish meanings, who care about Jewish traditions, who live by the Jewish calendar. Such Jews are Reform, Conservative, Reconstructionist, and Orthodox. Not accidentally, such involvement and commitment reduces the amount of a family's bar and bat mitzvah-related stress. They see the bar and bat mitzvah ceremony as part of the natural Jewish rhythm of their lives.

Once a relatively peripheral ceremony in Judaism, bar and bat mitzvah have now moved to center stage of the consciousness of American Jews. They are the primary reason Jews even join synagogues. Parents say they want to give their children a "Jewish education," but their implicit (and often explicit) goal is for their child to complete her or his bat or bar mitzvah ceremony, and then play hooky from any further Jewish education. In virtually every Jewish community, there are even "bar mitzvah factories" where children can receive "quickie" bar mitzvah ceremonies—no synagogue membership required.

The American Jewish focus on bar and bat mitzvah is too often counterproductive. We define our goals too narrowly. The mechanics of managing the celebration—designing invitations, arranging the catering, dealing with relatives—consumes too much of our energy. So, too, does the goal of prowess in Hebrew, the demand that everything sound letter-perfect. It turns too many young people into expert lip-synchers of Torah and *haftarah*.

To most American Jews, bar and bat mitzvah is an *event.* It must become more of a *process,* part of an ongoing sense of becoming more Jewish, not only for the child but also for the family. More than this, we must recapture the long-lost sense of coherence between bar and bat mitzvah and the other moments of our Jewish lives. Inner meaning, spirituality, and such venerable Jewish values as study, justice, giving, sanctity, moderation can become more real as a result of bar and bat mitzvah. We should focus not *only* on reading the Torah, but also on *hearing* the Torah as uniquely addressed to us, in our time, in our place.

The bar and bat mitzvah ceremony presents a challenge to today's scattered and sometimes fractured families. Guests and family members are often not clear about the meaning of the service and how to participate in it. The family of the bar or bat mitzvah child is often caught in the ethics of celebration—and in the highly subjective matter of "good taste." Bar and bat mitzvah ostentation has become a morally debilitating part of the American Jewish landscape, though many families have rebelled admirably against the culture of glitz. Their experiences prove that this trend can be reversed, that the celebration can be kept in perspective, that the sense of spirituality that is inherent in the ceremony can be reclaimed.

Judaism's teachings on contemporary moral issues encapsulate Torah's goal—to shape us into better human beings. What wisdom does Judaism offer our young people as they enter maturity? And how do we keep them learning from this wisdom? It is precisely for this reason that Jewish life after bar and bat mitzvah presents a major challenge. Approximately fifty percent of all post-bar and bat mitzvah youths end their Jewish education at some point soon after the service. This disastrously affects the future Jewish identity of the child. Our young people lose access to Jewish wisdom on such issues as self-esteem and sexuality when they need it most.

Much of what happens in connection with bar and bat mitzvah is *spiritual sleepwalking*. To put it in terms that Menachem Mendl would have understood—some people just aren't *there*. That lack of spiritual presence is not unique to Jews. My Christian colleagues describe how many of their parishioners have lost or forgotten the meaning of first communion or confirmation. They speak of how these celebrations, too, have become secularized and distorted.

Several years ago in Paris, for instance, my wife and I eavesdropped on a baptism at the cathedral in Montmartre. As the priest recited the ancient words, the grandparents' faces were beaming. But the father had his hands shoved nervously into his pockets. His eyes were wandering across the stained glass. He wanted, it seemed, to be anywhere but there. He had forgotten the meaning of the moment.

And lest anyone think that Jews have a monopoly on adolescent coming-of-age parties, one need only look to the Hispanic American community where fifteen-year-old girls celebrate a mass called the *quinceanera* in which they are blessed and asked to affirm their dedication to the Church. A few years ago, priests in Phoenix were concerned that the ceremonies were beginning to dominate church schedules, that girls came to their ceremonies without the faintest idea of its religious significance, and that *quinceanera* parties had a "queen for a day" aura. To remedy this, Bishop Antonio Sotelo, the Bishop of Phoenix's Vicar for Hispanic Affairs, mandated classes on Bible study, Hispanic history, and modern morals. He also required church-sponsored retreats to prepare for the event.

Parents and their children acutely feel the social pressures that surround bar and bat mitzvah. But they want to feel the spiritual promise of the event, the pull of the divine, and the knowledge that they are participating in an event that has meaning both in the ancient past and in the very immediate present. They want to know that the steep incline before them is their family's own version of Sinai, the summit where, in every generation, Jews meet God, individually and as a people.

They want to know that bar and bat mitzvah can be a path to that summit. And they want to know how to get there.

This book can be their guide.

At the end of each chapter, we've suggested some questions for you to consider. Our hope is that by addressing these questions, you will be able to truly "put God on the guest list," and that the words in this book will move from paper to reality.

C H A P T E R

1

Beyond "Today I Am A Man"

When I became bar mitzvah, my grandfather, Eleazar of Amsterdam, of blessed memory, came to me one night in a vision and gave me another soul in exchange for mine. Ever since then, I have been a different person.

—SHALOM OF BELZ, HASIDIC MASTER

Beyond "Today I Am A Man"

Bar and bat mitzvah is what a young person *becomes,* simply by becoming thirteen (or in Orthodox synagogues, twelve for girls). It is not an event or ceremony. It is not a verb, as in "The rabbi bar mitzvahed my son." Bar and bat mitzvah literally translates as "son or daughter of the commandment." What it really *means* is "old enough to be responsible for *mitzvot.*" Mitzvot are the commandments that a Jew does in order to not only live a *Jewish* life, but also to *sanctify* life.

How Did Bar Mitzvah Begin?

Abraham, Moses, David—none were a bar mitzvah. Biblical tradition placed the age of majority at twenty. This was the age of mandatory army service and of priestly service. So bar mitzvah, as a concept, actually emerged during the first centuries of the Common Era. It is an invention of the early rabbis, the sages whose interpretations of Torah created contemporary Judaism. We cannot be absolutely sure why these sages lowered the age of majority from twenty to thirteen, though certainly the connection to the age of puberty has some significance. When the term "bar mitzvah" appears in rabbinic literature, it simply refers to a young man who has reached the age of thirteen plus one day.

If anyone could be called the "inventor" of bar mitzvah, it would be the second century, C.E. sage, Judah ben Tema. Judah envisioned the way that one's life of Jewish study and responsibility should unfold: "At five, one should study Scripture; at ten, one should study Mishnah; at thirteen, one is ready to do *mitzvot;* at fifteen, one is ready to study Talmud; at eighteen, one is ready for the wedding canopy; at twenty, one is responsible for providing for a family" (Mishnah, *Avot* 5:24).

Most references to the significance of the age of thirteen come from stories the rabbis told about characters in the Bible. At thirteen,

Abraham smashed the idols in his father's house (Midrash, *Pirkei De-Rabbi Eliezer* 16). At thirteen, the twins, Jacob and Esau, went their separate ways—Jacob to the worship of God, Esau to idolatry (Midrash, *Bereshit Rabbah* 63:10).

Thirteen: The Age Of Choices

As the years progressed, a certain prayer, *Baruch she-petarani me-onsho shel zeh* ("Blessed is the One Who has now freed me from responsibility for this one") was recited by fathers when their sons became bar mitzvah. While the true meaning of this blessing has been debated for some time, most agree that it means that the father is no longer responsible for his son's sins.

But it is also a kind of cosmic sigh—an admission that even sincere, competent, highly committed parents are limited in what they can do with their children. The rest is up to the child himself or herself. When parents say *Baruch she-peterani,* they say, in effect, "Whatever this young person does now, he is legally and morally culpable. Thank God, it's not my responsibility."

Thirteen was the age of spiritual and moral choices. The *midrash* says that at the age of thirteen, Abraham looked into the heavens and concluded there was a God. Some rabbinic sources say that only at the age of thirteen is a youth first able to make mature choices, because at that time the child becomes endowed with both the *yetser hatov* (the good inclination) and the *yetser hara* (the evil inclination), the dueling forces that Jewish theology places within the human psyche.

Thirteen was also the age of religious achievement. According to the Talmud, Bezalel, the architect of the Tabernacle and namesake of Jerusalem's famous art school, was thirteen when he designed the desert sanctuary. The thirteen-year-old child could help constitute a *minyan* (the quorum of ten adult men needed for communal prayer).

Thirteen also became the age of a kind of legal maturity. The Mishnah, the code of Jewish law compiled around 200 C.E., considers the vows of a boy aged thirteen and a day as legally *binding*. At thirteen, a youth could be a member of a *beit din* (a Jewish court), and could buy and sell certain items of value, though apparently not real estate.

The age of thirteen was therefore the crossroads of spiritual, moral, and religious maturity.

There is yet another opinion about the origin of bar mitzvah. Bar mitzvah may have its roots in the *berit milah* (ritual circumcision) ceremony that occurs when a boy is eight days old. At that ceremony, the father says, "As we have brought this child into the covenant of Abraham, so, too, will he be brought into the study of Torah, the *chupah* [the wedding canopy] and the performance of good deeds." Bar mitzvah was, therefore, the occasion when the community confirmed that the father had fulfilled the first part of the promise. Ideally, the same people who had attended the *berit* would also be present when the child became bar mitzvah.

Bar mitzvah, therefore, was a passage not only for the child, but also for the father. In modern times, it is a passage for both parents. It meant that they had fulfilled their Jewish responsibility to the child and to the Jewish community.

How Did Bar Mitzvah Customs Evolve?

A child who was younger than thirteen years old performed *mitzvot* as *options*. Once he turned thirteen, they were performed as *obligations*. As the Talmud taught, "It is better to do something when you're commanded to do so than to do something when you're *not* commanded to do so." The idea of *mitzvah* also implies responsibility and obligation. It connects us to the covenant of Abraham, Isaac, and Jacob, of Sarah, Rebecca, Rachel and Leah, and of all Jews who preceded each thirteen-year-old. It is sacred and it deserves celebration.

Jews sensed this, and during the early Middle Ages, practices began to change. In the twelfth century, the religious rights of minors began to disappear. We are not sure why this occurred. Perhaps it was because the carnage of the Crusades had created a shortage of men, and Jewish communities wanted to give them top priority in ritual matters.

By approximately the late Middle Ages, minors could no longer wear *tefilin* (phylacteries) or be called for *aliyot* to the reading of the Torah. Since those rituals became the defining elements of Jewish maturity, they later became the essential features of the bar mitzvah observance. In the sixteenth century, it became customary to call a boy to read the Torah on the Shabbat that coincided with or followed his thirteenth birthday. He read the last section of the Torah *(maftir)* that was read on that particular Shabbat and also the weekly section from the Prophets section of the Hebrew Bible *(haftarah)*. Previously, the right of the minor to read the *haftarah* had not been restricted except on a few special Shabbatot.

Historically, bar mitzvah was a somewhat peripheral ceremony. But there were several exceptions even before modern times. The most poignant was the Marranos, those Jews of Spain who converted to Christianity under duress, but secretly maintained certain Jewish practices and beliefs. Bar mitzvah became a crucial time for Marrano families. It was the moment when they informed the child that he was Jewish. If he had been informed of this earlier, his immaturity might have prevented him from keeping it as well-guarded a secret as it had to be. Yet, if he had learned *later* than this, then the Christian element of his identity would have "taken," making any kind of link to Judaism much more difficult.

A Custom, Not A Commandment

If anything celebrates the diversity of Jewish expression, it is bar and bat mitzvah. The reason for this is clear—they are customs with no force of law. Standard in a bar or bat mitzvah ceremony, however, is the practice of the young person reciting the blessings for the Torah, reading or chanting that week's Torah portion, and reading the *haftarah* from a printed sheet. In the late Middle Ages, it became customary for the bar mitzvah to offer a *derashah* (sermonette or discourse) in the home. That *derashah* has been transformed into the bar mitzvah speech, which usually serves as a *devar Torah* (a sermonette on the Scriptural lesson) or as a personal prayer for the occasion. In many synagogues, the young person also leads the congregation in the Hebrew prayers in the service. In most synagogues, parents, grandparents, and other closer relatives are given *aliyot* and other honors. While most bar mitzvah ceremonies occur during regular worship on Shabbat morning, Friday evening bar mitzvah ceremonies are not uncommon.

Bar And Bat Mitzvah As American Judaism's Spiritual Mirror

Bar and bat mitzvah mirrors spiritual trends in American Judaism. Take, for instance, "privatization"—the focus on the individual and the resulting diminishing of religious community. We see this in Reform Judaism's Shabbat morning service being almost totally dedicated to the bar and bat mitzvah ceremony. This is certainly less so in Conservative, Reconstructionist, and Orthodox Judaism, in which the bar mitzvah ceremony is part of a service that would have been held whether or not there was a bar or bat mitzvah ceremony. We see this in the growth of Saturday evening bar and bat mitzvah ceremonies in Reform synagogues—the so-called *"havdalah"* bar and bat mitzvah which are held in conjunction with the service that ends Shabbat.

But mainstream opinion discourages such *havdalah* ceremonies. The reasoning is clear—the Torah is not traditionally read at that time; the timing of such ceremonies puts undue emphasis on the Saturday evening festivities; and *havdalah* bar and bat mitzvah ceremonies convince people that the service is "theirs," diminishing the centrality of the community in Jewish life.

Another trend is the growth of the American Jewish civil religion. This religious expression has little to do with theology. Instead, it is based on the trauma of the Holocaust; financial, political, and emotional support of Israel; philanthropy and political action; and concern with Jewish survival as a nebulously defined goal in itself which is often separated from other Jewish religious values and beliefs.

Bar and bat mitzvah have been put into service toward supporting this secular Jewish religion. During the dark days of Soviet Jewish oppression, American Jewish children would become pen-pals with the children of Soviet Jewish "refuseniks," then symbolically link their bar and bat mitzvah ceremonies with those children. Empty chairs on the *bimah* would be set for those refusenik children, and they would be called in absentia for *aliyot*. I know several American Jewish teenagers who ultimately visited with their Russian "twins," who were then living in the United States or in Israel. Increasingly popular has been twinning with Ethiopian Jewish children, the most recent Jews to settle in Israel. Such "twinning" usually entails some kind of financial help for Ethiopian Jews in Israel, rather than a pen-pal relationship.

Another manifestation of this secular Jewish religion is holding the bar and bat mitzvah ceremony in Israel. There is no question that such ceremonies create an unbreakable bond between the child and Israel. For many years the favored site was the Western Wall. This has become less popular because of the enforced separation of women at the Wall. An increasingly popular site for the ceremony is now the excavated synagogue at Masada, the Herodian palace overlooking the Dead Sea where the last Zealots held out against the Romans (73 C.E.). Masada symbolizes Jewish continuity in the face of hatred.

In many quarters of American Jewish life, bar and bat mitzvah still primarily means a youth can participate in rituals and he or she is responsible for *mitzvot*. As an Orthodox rabbi noted:

> If their bar mitzvah speeches are any indication, my students really do believe that they are now supposed to perform *mitzvot*. I hear them saying, "Once I would try to fast as long as I could on Yom Kippur as an option. Now I do it as a responsibility." They now have to wear *tefilin*. They can now help make a *minyan*. Becoming bar mitzvah has a sense of immediacy with my people. There's a tangible change in status.

But in less traditional American Jewish circles, bar and bat mitzvah have other meanings. These may not be explicitly theological. But bar and bat mitzvah means, in all forms of contemporary Judaism, that Judaism survives *in this family* and by implication, in the world at large. Making that survival coherent and meaningful is our task.

How Did Bat Mitzvah Begin?

Starting in the second or third century of the Common Era, Jewish girls at the age of twelve had a legal responsibility to observe *mitzvot*. It was not until centuries later, however, that families would begin celebrating the girl's new status with some festivity.

By the 1800s, some families held a *seudat mitzvah* (a festive meal for a ritual occasion) on a girl's twelfth birthday. Sometimes the girl would deliver a talk and her father would recite the traditional *Baruch she-petarani* prayer.

Bat mitzvah has always been controversial among Orthodox Jews. Some believe that its status should be less than bar mitzvah because girls must be more demure than boys. Others realize that sound educational arguments support the custom of bat mitzvah.

In mainstream Orthodoxy, the bat mitzvah ceremony is basically a sermonette on the Torah portion, followed by a festive meal. Sometimes the girl does the *devar Torah* in the sanctuary, sometimes in the social hall. Girls are seldom allowed to read directly from the Torah scroll. In some Orthodox synagogues, girls lead the service and read from either the Prophets or Writings sections of the Bible. In Orthodoxy, bat mitzvah services may be held on Friday evening, Saturday evening, or Sunday morning, or even after the regular weekday morning service.

The first bat mitzvah ceremony in North America was Judith Kaplan Eisenstein's, the daughter of Rabbi Mordecai Kaplan, the founder of Reconstructionism. It happened in May, 1922, when, she later recalled, she was "midway between my twelfth and thirteenth birthdays."

Years later, she would remember that the night before the event, her father had still not decided the exact form of the ceremony. The next day, as usual at a Shabbat service, Rabbi Kaplan read the *maftir* (the concluding portion of the Torah reading) and the *haftarah*. Then his daughter, "at a very respectable distance" from the Torah scroll, recited the first blessing and read the Torah selection from her own *chumash* (a book containing the Pentateuch).

"That was it," she later wrote. "The scroll was returned to the ark with song and procession, and the service was resumed. No thunder sounded, no lightning struck. The institution of bat mitzvah had been born without incident, and the rest of the day was all rejoicing."

Neither Reform Judaism nor Reconstructionist Judaism liturgically distinguish between bar mitzvah and bat mitzvah. In Conservative Judaism, practices range from the girl leading the service and reading from the Torah scroll to simply reading the *haftarah*. The time of the service might also vary. Some Conservative synagogues let a girl publicly celebrate becoming bat mitzvah on Shabbat morning. Others limit it to Friday evenings, or Monday, Thursday, and *rosh chodesh* (the first day of the Hebrew month) mornings when the Torah is also read.

Adult Bar And Bat Mitzvah

Recent decades have seen the growth of the phenomenon of adult bar and bat mitzvah. In particular, adult women, who were not bat mitzvah when they turned thirteen, have taken upon themselves the *mitzvah* of Jewish and Hebrew study and "become" bat mitzvah later in life. (The term is somewhat of a misnomer, as a child becomes bar or bat mitzvah at thirteen, regardless of whether or not a formal ceremonial marker of the passage takes place).

Usually, adults who become bar or bat mitzvah lead a service or sections of it, read Torah and/or *haftarah,* and give a *devar Torah.* Adult bat mitzvah in particular has become an important part of the continuing education programs of many synagogues. For women who are literate in Judaism, it offers the opportunity to affirm their active role in the ritual life of Judaism in a way that they could not do when they were thirteen.

What, Finally, Does It All Mean?

I believe that most Jewish parents need to turn inward and ask themselves these thorny questions: "Why are we doing this? What does it all mean?" To my frustration, I have discovered that many parents and children have never discussed the meaning of bar and bat mitzvah with each other. What results is a ceremony that is essentially a performance, a demonstration of rudimentary linguistic competence in an ancient language, and woefully little attention is paid to the underlying meaning and beauty of it all.

And yet, one thread links all the bar and bat mitzvah ceremonies of history, all the comings of age of every Jewish boy from Abraham on and every Jewish girl from Sarah on. Bar mitzvah and bat mitzvah are a passage, but not one of puberty. "It's when I become a man," say too many bar mitzvah candidates. Curiously, bat mitzvah girls rarely say,

"It's when I become a woman." Instead, they say, "Bat mitzvah is when I get new responsibilities." And they are right.

Bar and bat mitzvah is about ritual maturity. It is about growing up as a Jew. It is about becoming a fuller member of the Jewish community. But it is also about moral responsibility, about connecting to Torah, to community, to God.

Have each person in your family write down what he or she thinks bar or bat mitzvah should mean. Then, come up with a family definition for bar or bat mitzvah and write it below. It will become a wonderful memento for your child.

The River of Tears
Why Parents And Grandparents Cry At
Bar And Bat Mitzvah Ceremonies

May you live to see your world fulfilled
May your destiny be for worlds still to come,
And may you trust in generations past and yet to be.
May your heart be filled with intuition
and your words be filled with insight.
May songs of praise ever be upon your tongue
and your vision be a straight path before you.
May your eyes shine with the light of holy words
and your face reflect the brightness of the heavens . . .

—TALMUD, BERACHOT 17A

The River of Tears

There is no such thing as a bar or bat mitzvah ceremony without tears.

The tears belong to several people. They belong to parents who are swelling with pride and relief. They belong to grandparents who may come up for their *aliyah*. They listen to their grandchild read or chant from the Torah, and by the time they utter the closing blessing, their lips are quivering and their tears are falling. I have seen tears fall right onto the Torah scroll. Of all the places where tears might fall, that is the holiest place of all.

Sometimes I tell the bar and bat mitzvah children about the River of Tears. It is an ancient legend that I invented.

There is a River of Tears at every bar or bat mitzvah ceremony. By definition, tears are salty. This River of Tears is sweet. This river flows with the tears of parents who have heard their children read from Torah. It is a very powerful river, for it is a very ancient river. It is a river that began in ancient Israel, and then flowed to Babylonia, and then to Spain and France and Germany and Poland and the United States and South Africa and Israel and Argentina. It is a river that flows from generation to generation. It is a river that flows wherever Jews have lived and worshipped. It gets mightier and sweeter with every passing Shabbat.

What is the source of these holy tears? What is it about bar and bat mitzvah that moves even "un-religious" Jewish parents and grandparents so deeply?

Tribal Tears

Tribal memory unleashes the tears. We Jews are a tribe, in the highest and best sense of the word. Bar and bat mitzvah is the moment in the Jewish life cycle that most deeply defines who Jews are as a tribe. The Torah is their tribal wisdom.

Throughout history, the Jewish people have felt a sense of exile, and the Torah is our portable ancestral homeland. The Psalmist of almost two thousand years ago knew the feeling well: "By the waters of Babylon, we lay down and wept when we remembered Zion . . . How can I sing the song of the Eternal in a strange land?" (Psalm 137: 1,4).

Many American Jews, in particular, live with a sense of separation from a past once loved and now lost. Our exile is not only geographic, a function of living outside the land of Israel. It is spiritual. We live in a strange land of modernity, a land of dwindling communities and a land without social boundaries. Yet we want to retrieve that sense of rootedness that we, as a people, had when we sang the Lord's song. Its notes may have changed, but it is still, we sense deeply, very much the song of the Lord. And it can still, we sense deeply, console and reassure.

A few years ago, the Dalai Lama, the spiritual leader of Tibet, met for the first time with Jewish leaders and teachers. He had one main question for them: "How have you managed to live for so long in exile from your homeland?" He hoped the answer would guide and inspire him as he led the scattered, demoralized, exiled Tibetan people. Our teachers told him that we Jews had brought into exile our values (such as righteousness, mercy, compassion, justice), our holy books (such as the Torah and the Talmud), and our ideas and ideals of the family.

The peak moments of life, when we experience the drama of passage, have an uncanny way of bringing us home. They can take us out of exile and show us the Jerusalem of the soul. They remind us that our lives have a rhythm and a purpose. The Protestant theologian, Archie Smith, once defined worship as the act of forgetting that you've forgotten. That is one reason for worship. To forget that we have forgotten. To forget that we are in exile from our roots. To reclaim our links to Jewish memory.

Judaism structures time and events for the Jew, the Jewish family, and the Jewish people. We could celebrate our thirteen-year-old child's birthday with a large party and a football game. Instead, we practice the teachings of our tribal wisdom because they give us rhythm and structure. They are like a grid superimposed over the chaos of existence.

It is not only at bar or bat mitzvah that we feel the sense of structure amidst chaos. It is also how Kaddish, the prayer for the dead, functions. "Precisely at a time of our lives when we are most easily vulnerable to the threat of meaninglessness and chaos, our religious tradition gives us a ritual that puts order back into our lives in a very concrete way," Rabbi Neil Gillman, the eminent Conservative theologian, wrote.

In the nineteenth century, the so-called Bog Irish found themselves living in London. Remembering the traditions of their Catholic childhood in Ireland, they abstained from eating meat on Fridays. Such abstinence once symbolized personal mortification. It was a small weekly remembrance of the crucifixion of Jesus. Today, the meatless Friday may have lost its theological meaning for most Catholics, but it still means something to the Bog Irish. It represents a longing for a homeland, a sense of being in exile.

What an anthropologist wrote about the determination of the Bog Irish to observe meatless Fridays could just as well have applied to why certain Jews observe certain traditions: "If a people takes a symbol that originally meant one thing, and twists it to mean something else, and energetically holds on to that . . . symbol, its meanings for their personal life must be very profound."

For many Jews, the Torah once symbolized divine revelation. Since modern Jews have transformed it into something else—tribal memory, roots, order over chaos—its meaning for our lives must be very profound.

Immortal Tears

The River of Tears flows because of a sense of immortality.

Personal immortality is the unspoken, unarticulated prayer at every life cycle event. The prolific Talmudic scholar, Rabbi Jacob Neusner, spoke for many of us when he wrote: "At a bar or a bat mitzvah, a parent thinks not so much of the future as of the past, especially if a grandparent or a parent is deceased; the entire family one has known has assembled, and that is as much the past as the future."

At some level, often one that is deep and inarticulate, we know this. I remember a particular bat mitzvah in my last congregation. The father of the bat mitzvah had never struck me as a particularly emotional man, but at that service, standing over the Torah, he wept profusely. Standing next to him at the reading table, I was bewildered. Weeks later he told me why he had cried. "My father and my brother are both deceased. My kids are named for both of them. And now my daughters are both mature Jewish adults. I felt that the cycle was complete. Certain things touch you that persuade you of a Higher Power. For me, it was the memory of people who had died. I tell you, I could hear them taking pleasure in my daughter reading the Torah."

We know that our loved ones are immortal. We know that there is something intangible called the soul that spans time and space. As the soul is to the individual body, so the Torah is to the Jewish people. It is the soul of the Jewish people. When we share moments of Torah, we guarantee the immortality of the Jewish people.

That dream of immortality for the Jewish people is as ancient as Ezekiel's vision of a valley of dry bones—the Jewish people after the destruction of Jerusalem in 586 B.C.E., miraculously coming back to life. Modern Jews, too, have seen dry bones come back to life. To the parents and grandparents of the generation after the Holocaust, the bar and bat mitzvah ceremony symbolizes that they are not the last Jews on earth. More than our mere ethnicity, reading from the Torah at bar and bat mitzvah guarantees our immortality as a people.

When the Romans executed the sage, Chananya ben Teradyon, in the second century, they tied him to the stake with a Torah scroll and lit the pyre. As the smoke curled around him, his disciples asked him, "Our teacher, what do you see?"

Lifting up his eyes and his voice, he uttered his last words: "The scroll is burning, but the letters are returning to heaven."

Scrolls have burnt. The letters of the Torah always return to heaven. Unfailingly, they always return to us as well, replenishing us, restoring us, and keeping us alive as a people.

Mid-life Tears

The tears flow because we are moved by what is happening within *us,* the parents. The contemporary Jewish theologian, Richard Rubenstein, wrote that bar and bat mitzvah ceremonies are the occasion of the parents' entry into middle age. Parents need rites of passage as much as their children do.

At the same time that children are going through their passage, their parents, who are usually just entering middle age, are pondering whether they are still useful and creative, or stagnating. In his classic *The Seasons of a Man's Life,* psychologist Daniel J. Levinson wrote that the task of mid-life is to discern the polarity between being young and being old and to wrestle with a sense of mortality and a wish for immortality. Mid-life is close to the median age of parents of children who are bar and bat mitzvah. In our maturing children, we see both our own aging, and our own immortality. We feel a greater sense of urgency to preserve through our children the values and traditions that we have cherished.

This transition occurs even on a purely mundane, social level. It may be the first time that many parents are hosting a large affair or are responsible for paying for such an event.

I recently spoke to a group of parents about how they experienced changes as a result of their child's bar and bat mitzvah.

Rabbi: For how many of you was this the first time that you had to do anything "grown up" in your family? When your children were born and there was a *berit milah* or a baby-naming, I imagine that sometimes your parents ordered the platters for the meal. But this is different, isn't it?

Parents (in unison): Yes!

Forty-year-old woman: I kept saying to myself, "You're too young for this." Just thinking that you have a thirteen-year-old child. You think back on the last time the whole family got together, which was for the *bris.* That was thirteen long years ago. And now we're back together again.

Forty-three-year-old man: We're not as old as our parents were when they did this.

Forty-five-year-old man: It made me realize how old I am and that my kids are not that young anymore. It made me grateful for the consoling bond of religion.

"It made me grateful for the consoling bond of religion." Such is the often unspoken power of religion—to guide us through our passages and to give us meaning.

Tears Of Passing Years

When grandparents bless the Torah at their grandchild's bar or bat mitzvah, they are often acutely aware of many things. They remember their own parents, which often means that they remember their own Jewish coming-of-age. They remember what it was like fifty, sixty, maybe seventy years before, when they were thirteen and their parents and grandparents stood over them. Many, if not most, of the grandmothers will not have those memories of becoming bat mitzvah. It matters little. They still feel the presence of their own parents and grandparents. Hence the tears.

The tears flow because they sense the irretrievable passing of the years. They are not young anymore. Neither, they realize, are their own children. As grandparents look into the twilight of their lives, they struggle against despair. Their generation is no longer dominant, and they are less vital or vibrant than before.

The Talmud teaches that to hear your child's child reading Torah is like hearing the words from Sinai itself. Grandparents, even those that call themselves "unreligious," cry when their grandchildren read Torah. They sense that their grandchildren are speaking words that evoke Sinai. The Austrian Jewish author, Stefan Zweig, once wrote: "One who looks at his father is like one who sees God, because he can look beyond his father to creation. And one who looks at his children sees God, because he can look beyond his children through the generations to the Messiah."

The River Of Sacred Time

There are two calendars of Jewish sacred time—the public and the personal. The public calendar of Jewish sacred time is the festival cycle. The private calendar of Jewish sacred time is the life cycle—birth, maturity, marriage, and death. With the exception of Rosh Ha-Shanah and Yom Kippur, Jewish spirituality has usually shifted from the festivals to the life cycle. When Jews experience *kedushah* (holiness), they invariably experience it in the life cycle—circumcision, baby-namings, bar and bat mitzvah, weddings, funerals.

Jewish spirituality has made this shift because Jews no longer share a common spiritual vocabulary. They lack a common Jewish language, with its inherited meanings, its sacred calendar, its poetry of word and gesture.

But also, society has shifted its focus from the group to the self. Individualism has triumphed. The only community that we usually know well is our family. The synagogue has become a place of public spaces and private meanings. The life cycle has become the place, then, when the Jew can experience "moment faiths," sacred moments in life when we realize that there is a God in the world.

With every life cycle experience, we can feel connected anew to the Jewish people, to God, to Torah. This helps us know that during those moments when we might feel personally adrift and in need of Judaism, our potent tribal wisdom is there for us. It is waiting for us, and is a salve for us.

At the *berit* ceremony, the *mohel* recites the words that God spoke to Abraham: *"Hithaleich lifanai veheyei tamim"* ("Walk before Me and be perfect"). Pointing to an empty chair, the *mohel* says, *"Zeh kisei shel Eliyahu hanavi, zachur latov"* ("This is the chair of Elijah, the prophet of blessed memory"). Elijah is "there" to assure that the covenant lives. The *mohel* has already evoked Abraham, the first Jew. Elijah, the harbinger of the Messiah, is the last Jew. The newborn infant may yet be the Messiah, or may help usher in the Messianic Age. History and the Jewish people live through this child. Torah, also, potentially lives as well.

So, too, with the wedding, which is more than two people celebrating and confirming their love. It is the reprise of the covenant between God and Israel. The bride and groom are no longer themselves. The seven wedding blessings urge the couple to imagine themselves as Adam and Eve, cradled yet again in the Garden of

Eden. The blessings end by proclaiming that the marriage may help bring the Messianic Age. The groom's shattering of the glass is most frequently interpreted as a memory of the destruction of the Temple in Jerusalem, a further link to Jewish history and experience.

Even at death, the larger historical community is present. At a funeral service, usually a passage is read from Psalms, the oldest written Jewish liturgy. Then comes Kaddish, part of the inherited spiritual repertoire of every Jew, no matter how estranged. And finally, the service ends with the community saying to the mourners: *Hamakom yenachem etchem betoch shear avelei Tzion viYerushalayim* ("May God comfort you among those who are mourners for Zion and Jerusalem"). The liturgy links across space and across time the individual mourner's anguish to that of the larger Jewish people.

At the bar and bat mitzvah ceremony, the visible and, even, the invisible generations are present, just as they were present for the sealing of the covenant. The silent, implicit message of bar or bat mitzvah is the revelation that each parent understands: *I am not the last Jew in the world.*

Knowing that the youth before us embodies all that passed before him or her, that this thirteen-year-old incarnates Jewish triumphs, tragedies, wisdom, virtues, and the soaring hopes of a people who have seen themselves decimated only to rise again from the blackest of ashes, the River of Tears flows unendingly from one bar or bat mitzvah to another. It is a constant reminder of Jewish yesterdays that were fulfilled or frustrated, and of Jewish tomorrows still to come.

What are your feelings as your child prepares to become bar or bat mitzvah? What changes are you going through at this time? How do you think Judaism can help you get through the different cycles of life? Write your answers here.

CHAPTER

3

Hearing God's Voice

The Meaning Of Torah

The divine word spoke to each and every person according to his or her particular capacity: the young according to their capacity, the old in keeping with their capacity . . .

—MIDRASH, *Pesikta de Rav Kahana*

Hearing God's Voice

Something uplifting, something inarticulately holy occurs when a child reads from the Torah scroll on the day when he or she becomes bar or bat mitzvah.

Like many words from religious traditions, Torah has multiple meanings. It literally means "teaching." When we speak of reading from the Torah, we generally mean reading from the *sefer Torah,* the Torah scroll itself. The scroll contains the Five Books of Moses. Each book has a name in Greek or English, and also a Hebrew name, which corresponds to the first or second words of the book. Therefore, Genesis, the Greek name, is *"Bereshit"* ("When God began to create") in Hebrew. Exodus becomes *"Shemot"* ("These are the names"); Leviticus is *"Vayikra"* ("And God called"); Numbers is *"Bemidbar"* ("In the wilderness"); and, Deuteronomy is *"Devarim"* ("The words").

What Torah Portion Will Your Child Read?

It takes a full Jewish year, starting in the fall with the festival of *Simchat Torah*, to read the Torah. Bar and bat mitzvah candidates read (or chant, according to the custom of their synagogue) the *parashah*, the Torah portion for that particular week.

If your child's thirteenth birthday falls roughly between mid to late September and the end of December, he or she will probably read from Genesis, which spans the years from the Creation to Joseph's death in Egypt. Much of the Hebrew Bible's richest narrative material is in Genesis—Creation, Cain and Abel; Noah and the Flood; and the tales of the patriarchs. It also includes the oldest complete novel in history, the story of Joseph, which takes up more than one-quarter of the book of Genesis.

If your child becomes thirteen between approximately January and the end of February, he or she will read a section from Exodus. This tells of the Jews' enslavement in Egypt; the rise of Moses and the liberation from slavery; the crossing of the Red Sea; the giving of the Ten Commandments; the idolatry of the Golden Calf; and the design and construction of the Tabernacle, the desert sanctuary for the original tablets of the Law. Exodus also includes various ethical and civil laws, such as the instruction "not [to] wrong a stranger or oppress him, for you were strangers in the land of Egypt."

If your child turns thirteen between approximately early March and the end of May, he or she will read a section of the book of Leviticus. The book contains the laws of sacrifice and purity and other Temple rituals, which were the responsibility of the tribe of Levi.

If your synagogue has summer bar and bat mitzvah ceremonies, your child who was born during June or July will read from the book of Numbers, which recounts the wanderings in the wilderness and various rebellions against the authority of Moses.

With the end of summer comes the end of the yearly reading of the Torah. Deuteronomy, the last book in the Torah, is essentially Moses' farewell address to the Israelites as they prepare to enter the land of Israel. Various laws that were previously discussed are repeated, sometimes with different wordings. Deuteronomy ends with the death of Moses on the summit of Mount Nebo as he looks across the valley into the land that he would not enter. On Simchat Torah, the scroll goes from the death of Moses to the creation of the world without missing as much as a breath.

What Else Is Torah?

The first part of the Hebrew Bible is the Torah. But there is much more to it than these five books. The accurate term for the Hebrew Bible is the *Tanach*, an acronym for *Torah, Neviim* (the Prophets) and *Ketuvim* (the later Writings). In Hebrew, the Torah is also referred to as the *Chumash*; in Greek, it is known as the *Pentateuch*. Both terms are derived from the word for "five" in their respective languages.

In the broadest sense, "Torah" means Judaism's entire literary and legal tradition. Studying Torah means not only studying *the* Torah (the *Chumash,* the *Pentateuch,* the Scroll), but the entire Hebrew Bible, as well. We can extend this to post-Biblical Jewish law and lore, such as the *Mishnah,* the *Talmud,* and the *Midrash,* and can speak even more broadly when we speak of studying Torah. We can mean studying medieval commentary, philosophy, poetry, mysticism, and Hasidism. We can mean studying modern scholars, teachers, and philosophers. We can mean *everything* that Jews have thought about, struggled with, and created during their history.

In effect, when we say *Torah,* we mean Judaism. We also mean anything that emerges out of our open encounter with those sources. As *Pirke Avot* (the ethical maxims of the early rabbis, as recorded in the *Mishnah*) says, "Every day a voice goes forth from Sinai." Every day, at least, if we can train our ears to hear the truth and the power and the beauty of the Torah.

Judaism is not just the words of the written Torah. It includes oral traditions as well. Jews are not fundamentalists. We do not lock ourselves into a prison of the text and exclude all external experience. Judaism has shaped and reshaped itself since its ancient days. Many of its practices have changed radically since Biblical days. For instance, Jews no longer celebrate Passover by sacrificing a lamb. The Torah tells us to refrain from working on the Sabbath and on the sacred days of the major festivals. Yet it never defines "work." Rituals that now seem essential to Shabbat—candle lighting and *kiddush*—are nowhere in the Torah. *Kippah* or *yarmulke,* traditional Jewish ritual head coverings, are not in the Torah. The Torah does not mention several holidays that we think are essential to Judaism, such as *Chanukah* and *Purim.* And it did not anticipate the Holocaust and the re-birth of the Jewish state, which have become pivotal to modern Jewish self-understanding.

Judaism begins with *the* Torah, the scroll that young Jews read as they become bar and bat mitzvah. Ideally, Torah becomes their Sacred Story, the lens through which they view themselves as Jews. These stories have survived because they are timeless.

Parents and children shudder when they hear the story of the binding of Isaac. The shuddering goes back to our very beginnings as a people. Every infertile couple inwardly weeps when hearing of Rachel's difficulty in bearing children. Her cry to her husband Jacob—"Give me children, or else I die!"—echoes across the centuries.

Single parents who struggle to raise children "know" the story of Hagar and Ishmael, Abraham's maidservant and her son, who were cast out into the desert. Everyone who has but an instant of spiritual enlightenment has been with Moses at the burning bush that was not consumed. Every Jew who has become successful while living in a non-Jewish culture knows what Joseph experienced in Egypt. And every aged person who hears the tale of the death of Moses knows what it is like to die before reaching one's greatest goal.

The modern German Jewish theologians, Martin Buber and Franz Rosenzweig, were absolutely right. Their translation of the Hebrew word for scripture, *mikra,* was *"calling out."* They knew that the Scriptures call out to each of us. If we listen carefully enough, quietly enough, knowledgeably enough, we will hear their call.

The Haftarah: The Rest Of God's Call To Us

The Scriptures are more than the Torah. After the Torah is read in the synagogue, the congregation hears the *haftarah,* which literally means "the conclusion." Haftarah comes from the *Neviim,* the Prophetic books, the second part of the Hebrew Bible, the *Tanach.* It is read from a Hebrew Bible, or in the case of a bar or bat mitzvah, sometimes from a photocopied sheet.

The Torah is read sequentially, from Creation to the death of Moses. But the *haftarah* is read selectively, from any number of prophetic and historical books. Those *haftarah* passages were chosen because of their thematic connection to the Torah text.

Not all books in the Prophetic section of the Hebrew Bible are prophecy. Several are historical. The Book of Joshua recounts the story of the conquest and settlement of Israel. Judges speaks of the time of anarchy when "no king ruled in Israel." Some judges are well-known through literature and history—Deborah, the great prophetess and military leader; Samson, the great Biblical strong man; Jephtah, who vowed to sacrifice the first animal (or person) that he saw after winning a decisive battle and sacrificed his only daughter.

The books of Samuel tell of the transition from the period of Samuel, the last judge and prophet, to the monarchy under Saul and

David. The books of Kings tell of the death of King David, the ascension of King Solomon, and the Israelite kingdom's rupture into the northern kingdom of Israel and the southern kingdom of Judah.

These historical books are noteworthy for, above all else, their striking sense of *normalcy*. Jews emerge as a holy people, but only in their potential. Their kings and generals are people of flesh and blood, with real-life urges, failures, weaknesses, and triumphs.

Then come the words of the prophets, those spokesmen for God whose words fired Jews' consciousness and conscience. Their names are immortal—Isaiah, Jeremiah, Ezekiel, Amos, Hosea. Their exhortations embody not the Jewish *story*, but Jewish visions—visions of the God that commands ethical behavior; visions that God chose the Jewish people *not* for privilege but for duty; visions of a hope that became the messianic promise of universal justice and peace, a sense that history is moving forward toward an ultimate, redemptive conclusion.

Why Your Child Reads Torah

Torah is more than the Scroll. It represents everything that Jews hold sacred.

Let us then consider: What is the significance of reading Torah during a worship service?

I once asked a group of parents of pre-bar and bat mitzvah candidates, "What does it mean for your child to read Torah when he or she becomes bar or bat mitzvah?" Among their responses:

- "That my son has completed his studies and achieved his goal that was taught in Hebrew and Sunday school."
- "He learns values from the Torah that can be applied to real life."
- "It signifies that she has come of age in the Jewish religion."
- "A link with his ancestors in a common bond that dates back for thousands of years."
- "A special moment in her life to read from such a special and sacred scroll."

There were more than a few answers of one word: "tradition."

I found the responses troubling. I read "skills" and "accomplishment" and "educated" and I wondered: How was this particular skill and accomplishment and educational achievement different from others that the child would experience?

One quality separates this act of learning, reading, and interpreting Torah to a congregation from all other experiences and learning and accomplishments. That quality is God.

Modern Jews are notoriously hesitant about speaking of God. They fear that accepting God as the source of Torah might lead to a dangerous flirtation with fundamentalism. "If God is in it, doesn't that mean God wrote it? If God wrote it, how can I even think of disagreeing with it?"

Jews have always perceived Torah through the eyes of great commentators and interpreters, such as Rashi, the great medieval sage who lived in the Rhineland in the eleventh century. Judaism treasured the idea that it must constantly reinterpret the tradition it had inherited. This is the opposite of fundamentalism, which believes in the unchanging, literal nature of a sacred scripture.

Consider the following famous legend from the Talmud. It teaches us about the greatness of the second-century sage, Rabbi Akiva. But it also speaks of the timeless nature of what is taught:

> When Moses ascended Sinai, he found God attaching little crowns to the letters of the Torah.
>
> "Master of the Universe," asked Moses, "why are You attaching these crowns?"
>
> "Someday in the future," replied God, "a man will appear named Akiva ben Joseph who will be able to make heaps of interpretations based on these little crowns."
>
> "Let me see him," said Moses.
>
> "Turn around," said God.
>
> Moses found himself listening to a class in Akiva's academy. But he could not understand what was going on and he was distressed.

Finally a certain subject came up and the students asked Akiva, "How do you know this?" and Akiva replied, "This is a teaching from Moses on Sinai." And Moses was pleased . . . (Talmud, *Menachot* 29b).

Akiva could look into what he was teaching and find the echoes of what Moses heard on Sinai. If we can train our ears, so can we.

To restore sanctity to bar and bat mitzvah, we need to link that event with the moment at Sinai when Moses received the tablets. Like Akiva, we must find ourselves in the letters of the Scroll. Our children must feel that they, like Moses, are standing at the foot of their own private Sinais.

You may wonder whether it is enough to believe that Torah is the great literature of a great people. That position is common and respectable. That is what college students learn when they take courses on "The Bible as Literature." As literature, Torah is, indeed, wonderful. But *simply* as literature, it becomes as spiritual as, say, Mark Twain. It loses its fire and its passion.

Traditional Judaism holds that God dictated the entire text of Torah to Moses. This view sees revelation as a singular event, not a constantly evolving process.

There are, of course, other views. Modern scholarship sees the development of literary traditions within the Torah itself. Yet, this knowledge hardly detracts from the sanctity of what we read. Similarly, we do not need to know exactly how Picasso chose to paint *Guernica* to feel the full impact of the painting.

Where do we get this sense that God is *in* the text, even if we believe that God did not write the text?

God's Presence In The Scroll

The Torah is great literature. Shakespeare and Tolstoy are also great literature. So is Dickens, yet no contemporary Englishman would open *Oliver Twist* to find spiritual uplift in its pages. The *Odyssey* is great literature, yet we cannot imagine a modern Greek running into a burning building to rescue a manuscript of it, as generations have done for the Torah scroll. If we were to look at the Torah as simply the great literature of our people, then it would not command or move us as it does.

The fact that we American Jews use the Torah scroll indicates that we have not become entirely secularized. We Jews understand, often purely intuitively, the power of the Scroll. It evokes history, continuity, tradition—and it does so in a way that no other Jewish ritual object can.

Consider, first, the *halachah* (traditional Jewish law) regarding how a Torah scroll must be treated. There is one law that almost every Jew knows: a person who accidentally drops a Torah scroll must atone through fasting or giving charity. Some say the person who witnesses the dropping of the Torah must also fast as an act of mourning. As the late scholar Rabbi Daniel J. Silver wrote, the Torah "had become revelation, resplendent in divine mystery, symbol and substance of God's wisdom, the source too holy to be handled with any but the most reverent humility." The Nazis delighted in desecrating Torah scrolls and transforming them into profane objects, such as shoes and, even, a banjo. Photographs from *Kristallnacht* of November, 1938 show thugs unraveling Torah scrolls out of synagogue windows. On that Night of Broken Glass, countless Jews ran back into burning synagogues to rescue Torah scrolls. Some of those Jews were learned; some were religiously ignorant. But they all felt the pull of the Scroll, the same pull that every generation of Jews had felt dating back to Sinai.

How Do We Experience God In The Service?

The liturgical high moment of Shabbat morning worship is the Torah service. And the emotional "center" of that service occurs when the Torah is removed from the *aron hakodesh* (the Holy Ark). What is the Ark? And what does it mean to Jews?

To Daniel J. Silver, a divine choreography is performed before the Ark. The curtain in front of the Ark, he explained, recalls

> . . . in purpose and name, the *parochet,* the curtain that had fronted the Holy of Holies in the Temple, where the ark containing the Tablets of the Ten Commandments was said to have been kept . . .

and where in the Second Temple there had been an empty space filled with God's presence. . . . The *sefer Torah* was understood as God's immanent presence. Men bowed when they crossed in front of the Ark and rose when it was opened, because of its sacred contents.

But the Ark itself has even greater significance. Anthropologist Joseph Campbell wrote that sacred stories connect us to sacred places. Each culture believes that its sacred place is the center of the earth. Jews are no exception. The Holy of Holies in the ancient Temple on the Temple Mount in Jerusalem was the very navel of the earth. It was where the tablets of the covenant were kept. Some traditions say that place is the birthplace of Adam, or where Noah made his first sacrifice after the flood, or where Abraham bound Isaac as a sacrifice, or where Jacob dreamed of a ladder of angels. Moslems say it is where Mohammed ascended to heaven.

Since the ninth day of the Hebrew month of Av in the year 70 C.E.—the day the Romans destroyed the Temple—Jews have lacked this sacred center. But on each day the Torah is read—Monday, Thursday, Shabbat morning and afternoon, and festival mornings—Jews go before the Ark, the holiest spot in the holiest area in the holiest room in the holiest building that they know. And there, something happens.

What occurs when the rabbi removes the Torah from the Ark and prepares it for reading? More than meets the eye. The Ark in the synagogue "becomes" the Ark in the ancient Temple in Jerusalem. Every time the Torah is taken out to be read, Jews reenact the moment when God gave the Torah to Moses. In a sense, when a rabbi hands the scroll to a child, he or she re-creates the giving of the Torah to Moses to be read to the Jewish people.

The Scroll is held aloft after it is read or chanted and the congregation sings: "This is the Torah that Moses placed before the children of Israel to fulfill the word of God." Literary theorists suggest that the observers of such symbolic acts participate in an imaginative process called "the willing suspension of disbelief." It doesn't matter that the congregants saying these words may be sitting in a suburban synagogue wearing a suit or a dress. During services, we are united with all Jews everywhere in the world in all times. The synagogue may be only half full. But present is every Jew who has ever lived and who ever will live. For a few moments, when we stand at the open Ark, we are no longer in our synagogue. We stand before Sinai with our ancestors, witnessing the majestic and the awesome and the ineffable.

Note, finally, the magic of the Scroll itself. No parents would let their child read or chant his or her Torah portion from a printed page or even from a bound book. The Torah scroll is our link to the God who loves us and who made and keeps a Covenant with us.

Did God Write The Torah?

Because I believe in a pluralistic approach to Jewish sources, I believe that there are several ways of hearing God in the text. The first possibility is the supernaturalist interpretation regarding divine revelation. Most often called "Orthodox," this position states that God revealed the Divine Will at Sinai in both a written form (the written Torah, *Torah she-bichtav*) and oral form (*Torah she-be-al peh,* which was ultimately written down as the Mishnah and the Talmud). The oral tradition is the authoritative interpretation of the written Torah.

Rabbi Norman Lamm, president of Yeshiva University in New York, explained the Orthodox position in *The Condition of Jewish Belief:*

> The Torah is divine revelation in two ways: It is God-given and it is godly. By "God-given," I mean that He willed that man abide by His commandments and that that will was communicated in discrete words and letters. . . . I accept unapologetically the idea of the verbal revelation of the Torah. . . . *How* God spoke is a mystery; how *Moses* received this message is an irrelevancy. *That* God spoke is of the utmost significance.

Conservative Judaism, which occupies the centrist position in American Judaism, offers a spectrum of positions regarding God's role in revelation. Some Conservative theologians, such as the late Abraham Joshua Heschel, hold that God revealed the Divine Will at Sinai. Those revelations, however, were transcribed by human beings, which accounts for the wide variety of biblical traditions, and which also accounts for the occasional contradiction of these traditions.

Other Conservative theologians, such as the late Ben Zion Bokser, hold that *divinely inspired* human beings wrote down the Torah. Still others, such as the late Seymour Siegel, say Torah is the *human* record of the encounter between God and the Jewish people at Sinai. Since it was written by human beings, it contains some laws and ideas that we might reject as anachronistic.

In general, Conservative Judaism sees Torah as constantly evolving, yet rooted in a transcendent reality. It believes in *conserving* much of the traditional view of Torah, though accepting that our view of it is affected by the time in which we live. It looks at what Jews have done, at the practices they have abandoned, and approaches tradition while it is cognizant of contemporary realities. When changes are to be officially made, they must evolve through the Committee on Jewish Law and Standards of the Rabbinical Assembly, Conservative Judaism's rabbinic body.

Reconstructionist Judaism was the intellectual child of one of the most extraordinary Jews of the twentieth century, Rabbi Mordecai Kaplan (1881-1983). His writings also greatly affected the Conservative movement. Kaplan believed that Judaism was the creation of the Jewish community, influenced by the God who, existing within nature, cannot violate its laws. Kaplan also taught that Torah emerges from the life of the Jewish people.

Reconstructionists believe that revelation is the process by which the Jewish people discover God's purpose. The earliest record of this search is contained in the Torah. Ira Eisenstein, Kaplan's son-in-law and successor as the leader of the Reconstructionist movement, says in *The Condition of Jewish Belief:*

> Despite what the Torah claims for itself . . . I believe that it is a human document, reflecting the attempt of its authors to account for the history of the Jewish people, and for the moral and ethical insights which its geniuses acquired during the course of that history. It is "sacred literature" in the sense that Jews have always seen in it the source and the authority for that way of life and that view of history which gave meaning and direction to their lives.

Finally, there is the approach of contemporary Reform Judaism, expressed in the words of the Reform movement's *Centenary*

Perspective (1976): "Torah results from the relationship between God and the Jewish people." This approach owes a substantial debt to Franz Rosenzweig (1886-1929). Although this German Jewish layman died when he was only forty-three years old, he may have been the most influential Jewish thinker of our time. To Rosenzweig, the content of revelation is simply the *fact* that revelation occurred. At Sinai, God and the Jewish people met; at Sinai, God entered into a unique relationship with them.

It was an encounter without content. Torah, Rosenzweig explained, is Israel's classic response to that encounter. It is the creation of human beings who want to respond to that divine-human encounter. When we read Torah, and when we do Torah through the *mitzvot,* we respond to that encounter. "God is not a Law-giver," Rosenzweig wrote to Martin Buber in 1924. "But He commands. It is only by the manner of his observance that man changes the commandments into Law, a legal system with paragraphs."

Hearing God In The Torah: Sometimes It Is Very Easy

There are certainly moments when I hear the authentic voice of God—metaphorically—in the Torah. And I believe that those are moments when our young people can hear God's voice as well. There is little that compares with the opening words of the scroll: *Bereshit bara Elohim* ("When God began to create heaven and earth"). One does not have to be a fundamentalist to feel the power in this one sentence. It transcends geology and astronomy and suggests an order and a meaningfulness in the world. Since God made the world, *Bereshit* suggests that we who are made in God's image are stewards of God's creation. And since God included rest in the order of creation, Bereshit tells us that Shabbat is holy.

Many other stories with God's presence permeate the Torah. From them, our young people can find that God's voice truly sings forth—Abraham setting forth at God's command to a land that he did not yet know. The revelation of the Ten Commandments. Moses dying in solitude on Mount Nebo.

Why is God in those stories? Because their meaning has survived the centuries. Because they have an overwhelming literary beauty. Because of the emotions they elicit. And most often, because their implicit values have survived intact, though not unchallenged, into our time. When our young people interpret those stories and find their own place within those values, that is God's voice speaking once again.

Sometimes It Is Very Hard

Sometimes it is very hard to hear God in a text. But when young people try, in their trying they hear God telling them to strive for inspiration, to find the deeply imbedded jewel in a place that seems devoid of such jewels. When we seek to find meaning in a morally or aesthetically difficult text, we make a conscious effort to hear what the text might be saying to us. We are saying that there might be more wisdom before us than meets the eye. This is the essence of the Jewish search for wisdom—knowing that we do not have all the answers and believing that they may yet come through sincere inquiry and struggle.

I have two favorite examples of wisdom in unlikely places in the Torah. One is in Leviticus, which is a problematic book. Most of us Jews feel more connected to the Torah's stories than to its laws, and truth be told, there is really only one story, one *event* in the book. Fire consumes Aaron's sons, Nadav and Avihu, as they make the wrong kind of incense offering. An interesting story with some tantalizing commentaries, but, on the whole, not very uplifting.

That is the problem. Most of Leviticus is concerned with laws. It's one thing for our children to read the Torah's laws about compassion for strangers and widows and orphans, or to read the details of the construction of the Tabernacle. But the laws of Leviticus are something else again. Sacrifice. Blood. Altars. Purity. Impurity. Sexuality.

And then, there's the portion known as *Tazria,* sometimes combined with the subsequent portion *Metzora.* Here we encounter the Torah in all its real-life nakedness. Some bar or bat mitzvah candidate always gets this portion since it is almost impossible to "schedule" around it. This Torah portion "comes around" in the spring, the most popular season for a bar or bat mitzvah ceremony.

Consider the topics of *Tazria-Metzora*. Ritual impurity after child-birth. Menstrual flows. Various bodily emissions. A detailed description of a disease that may be leprosy or psoriasis. Yet, sometimes I hear some excellent bar and bat mitzvah speeches about this portion. Our teenagers are fascinated by the Torah's description of psoriasis and the accompanying social fear and ostracism. They integrate their growing sense of social justice and compassion into the words of the Torah portion. They know that the revulsion that the Torah describes is all too often identical to our contemporary revulsion as well to such diseases as cancer, epilepsy, AIDS. When our young people make the connection, Torah comes alive before their eyes. God has "spoken" again.

Genesis 34: The Rape Of Dinah

It had been the practice of my synagogue to let *benei mitzvah* choose the passages they want to read from the assigned Torah portion for their Shabbat. Jessica, a thirteen-year-old in my congregation, made a rather unusual choice. Her thirteenth birthday happened to fall in early December. *Parshat Vayishlach* from the book of Genesis was her Torah portion. *Vayishlach* contains several narrative gems, especially Jacob's wrestling with the unnamed stranger at the banks of the Jabbok River and his subsequent reunion with his brother, Esau. Yet, when presented with those literary options, she stunned me.

"No," she said, "I read the Torah portion and I want to read the part about Dinah. Didn't you once give a sermon about how she was raped? People should know about Dinah. I want to read her story."

Dinah? Hardly the story that a thirteen-year-old girl would want to share with friends and family. Reform synagogues do not read the entire Torah portion. They choose the Torah passage to be read on the basis of aesthetics and spiritual uplift. It may be years before the Torah scroll is opened to Genesis 34: "And Dinah, the daughter of Leah, went out to see the daughters of the land. Shechem, the son of Hamor the Hivite, prince of the land, saw her and he took her and he lay with her and he humbled her."

Apparently, Shechem loved Dinah and wanted to marry her. But first, Shechem's father, Hamor, had to agree that Shechem and all the males of his clan would be circumcised. On the third day after their circumcision, while they were still in pain, Simeon and Levi, Jacob's sons, slaughtered the men of Shechem and rescued their sister from Shechem's household.

On the day she became bat mitzvah, Jessica read the story of Dinah proudly and well. Jessica helped me understand that we can again redeem Dinah's story. We hear Dinah's voice frequently these days.

Some say that Dinah's story is not about rape, but about seduction. It is clearly about the place of one woman's sexuality in our sacred literature and in our imagination. Dinah says nothing in the story, and so the text is about the muteness of women and how this must be fought. The story is about violence and ethical profanation, themes that, regrettably, are alive and more than relevant today.

Jessica struggled with the tale of Dinah. In her *devar Torah,* she reminded the congregation that Dinah is silent and passive both in the Biblical tale and in more than a thousand years of rabbinic interpretation and retelling of her tale. She taught that Dinah's muteness symbolized the role of Jewish women in traditional society, a muteness that she thought must no longer exist. It was a sparkling morning of reclaiming Torah.

Young People Feel God

Through study or interpretation or teaching the congregation what he or she has learned, young Jews deeply and profoundly feel God in the Torah. I once asked a group of post- bar and bat mitzvah teens, "How did you feel the presence of God in your bar or bat mitzvah ceremony?" If you think that our children are entirely secularized and cynical, read how some young people answered me:

• "I felt that God was around when I held the Torah and when I was reading it. The Torah scroll symbolizes a special closeness to God."

• "Reading from the Torah was like God giving Moses the Torah. It's come down to us, and we're taking its laws into our hands. Because the Torah symbolizes God."

At such moments we understand the Torah blessing, *Baruch attah Adonai, notein hatorah,* "Blessed are You, Adonai, Giver of the Torah." God did not just give Torah at Sinai. God gives Torah *today.* This is Torah's magical potency that has spoken through the ages.

And that is what I say to the young person who is about to become bar or bat mitzvah, to a thirteen-year-old who is trembling, just as the Jews trembled when God revealed the Ten Commandments at Sinai. I hand the scroll to him or her and say: "Centuries ago, our people stood at Sinai. There in the wilderness, we met God. Centuries later, when we reflected on that presence and on that encounter, our people wrote these words that are found in this scroll. This scroll is the closest thing to what we know God wants of us. In this scroll are many of our stories, our laws, our teachings, even our very names. This scroll is the secret of our survival."

One more secret is that the scroll lets us hear God speak, either with hushed, comforting quiet or with a great cosmic peal that humbles. It is the way we hear God. It is the way we stand at Sinai once again. All that the Jewish people have been and all that we will be is on the *bimah* as a youth reads from the scroll. It is a scroll that has been battered and burned and torn through the ages. But it has survived because the Jewish people have cherished it.

Have each member of your family answer this question: What does Torah mean in my life? What do I believe the source of Torah to be? Come up with a family answer and write it here.

Putting The Mitzvah Back In Bar And Bat Mitzvah

God is hiding in the world.
Our task is to let the divine emerge
from our deeds.

—ABRAHAM JOSHUA HESCHEL, *God In Search of Man*

Putting The Mitzvah Back In Bar And Bat Mitzvah

Jewish children become bar or bat mitzvah because of God's covenant with the people of Israel. The *mitzvot* are our end of the covenant. *Mitzvah* is one of the most important ideas Judaism gave to the world: a relationship with God entails mutual responsibility. Traditionally, there are 613 *mitzvot* derived from the Torah. Ritual *mitzvot,* such as observing Shabbat and keeping the dietary laws of *kashrut,* connect us to God. Ethical *mitzvot,* such as not murdering or gossiping, govern our relationship with people. Some *mitzvot* are in positive language: "Thou *shalt.* . . ." Some mitzvot are in negative language: "Thou shalt *not.* . . ." The idea of *mitzvah* is central to Jewish identity. It is the essence of the Covenant, our end of the agreement made at Sinai, the summit of Jewish existence.

The Difference Between Mitzvah And Mitzveh

There is one problem with *mitzvah.* Many people don't know how to pronounce the word. There seem to be two pronunciations. Is it *mitzvah?* Or *mitzveh?*

One small vowel makes all the difference. *Mitzveh* is a Yiddish term that comes from the original Hebrew. Hebrew contributed almost 5,000 words to Yiddish, such as *chutzpah* ("audacity"), *ganif* ("thief"), and *maiseh* (from *maaseh,* "something that is done," a story). Yiddish often made slight changes in the original meaning of the Hebrew words. *Mitzveh* is a classic example. As author Moshe Waldoks once wrote, "*Mitzveh* encompasses moral deeds not explicitly enjoined by the religious teachings of Jewish tradition. *Mitzveh* means doing something for someone else; feeling communal solidarity by imitating God's concern for the world."

Mitzvah means something deeper. Traditionally, *mitzvot* are of divine origin. But somehow during the past century, we Jews lost the sense of *mitzvah* as a holy obligation. Meanwhile, *mitzveh* was alive and well, usually in casual Jewish conversation: "Why don't you do a *mitzveh* and call your great-uncle?" People rarely used the term *mitzveh* to mean something more binding than what you should do simply because it was a nice thing to do.

But as Rabbi Arnold Jacob Wolf of Chicago once said, "Judaism is more than the Boy Scout Handbook." It is more than niceness. To Judaism, *mitzvah,* obligation, is essential to Jewish living. It is a religious commandment, a link between God and humanity, a sacred obligation.

Sometimes we learn that what we thought was a *mitzveh* was really a *mitzvah.* My wife's grandmother would always take strangers off the streets into her home for Shabbat dinner. My mother-in-law thought that she was doing it because she was being nice; she was performing a *mitzveh.* A generation later, her daughter, my wife knew that a *mitzvah* was being enacted; she knew that a holy obligation had linked her grandmother to Jewish traditions.

Why Perform Mitzvot?

Traditional Judaism sees only one real reason to perform *mitzvot*—God commanded them through the Torah and through generations of Jewish legal literature (*halachah*) that describe *how* the *mitzvot* should be done.

Conservative, Reconstructionist, and Reform Judaism have produced many other reasons for doing *mitzvot.* Among these:

- *Mitzvot* are done to genuinely feel the Presence of God. Lighting Shabbat candles imparts a feeling of inspiration. *Havdalah,* the ceremony that ends Shabbat, uplifts us. Performing a *mitzvah* invites God into the human soul. Knowing that the *mitzvah* will continue to bring God's Presence is an impetus to do it again and again.

- *Mitzvot* are done because of what happened at Sinai. Sinai established a patterned way of Jewish life, a sense of discipline. Every *mitzvah* echoes that original Covenant. Jews perform righteous deeds not only because of the dictates of the conscience, but because an external force compels, a force that returns them to Sinai.

- *Mitzvot* are done to feel connected to Jews, past and present. History has a voice, and, to a Jew, *mitzvah* gives that voice its timbre, its weight. One Jew recently explained his refusal to eat pork precisely that way to me: "Sure, I like pork. I used to eat it. Then, I thought about the enemies of our people who forced us to eat pork as a kind of torture. In solidarity with those Jews, I stopped eating it."

- Finally, *mitzvot* are done because they connect Jews to Jewish tradition. That several-thousand-year-old tradition has produced some of Western civilization's greatest values. For that reason, they are not to be cavalierly disregarded or discarded. Shabbat, for example, can help restore the Jewish soul and also provide an oasis in time for the Jewish family. *Kashrut* can helped Jews retain their identity. By establishing limits to what we eat, it taught that there are boundaries in life, and kosher slaughtering taught avoiding unnecessary cruelty to animals. Torah study can be intellectually invigorating and soul-elevating. Space does not permit discussing all of the ethical *mitzvot,* such as business ethics, that are increasingly relevant with every passing year. Those *mitzvot,* at the very least, deserve the benefit of the doubt.

Just one of these reasons for doing *mitzvot* might be powerful enough to command more than simply "doing a good deed." But all four are compelling and persuasive. As the contemporary Jewish social commentator Leonard Fein said in *Where Are We? The Inner Life of American Jews:* "I am open to the language, to the question, and to the life of a Jew. I will not permit my problems with the tradition to separate me from it. I will enter the tradition, and its ritual elements, without a chip on my shoulder. The methods of the tradition have sustained very many people in very many places over centuries of time. So I must study. And wrestle. And listen. And err. And rejoice. And listen."

Mitzvah: The Torah's Active Voice

Mitzvot teach us to sanctify life. They foster altruism and self-esteem, so crucial to the life of a young Jew. They can bring Jewish families closer to the Jewish people, to all people, and to God.

Not each *mitzvah* will speak to every Jew. But each is sacred. So, too, is the idea that *what we do shapes who we are,* that the deed shapes the heart more than the heart shapes the deed. Most Jewish parents want their children to feel Jewish and to somehow be connected to the Jewish past and the Jewish future. Judaism teaches that only through the *doing* can there be a genuine, rooted, profound feeling of Jewishness.

A Jewish person's actions, then, create a Jewish world. Such actions have consequences. Perhaps the most powerful Jewish idea is *kiddush hashem,* which I choose to translate as "adding to the holiness of God's reputation." In some contexts, *kiddush hashem* means martyrdom for the sake of one's Jewish identity and Jewish ideals. But its deeper meaning is that when Jews act admirably, when Jews act like *menschen,* their lives serve as living testaments for God.

More than anything else, *that* is the goal of bar and bat mitzvah, and that is the goal of all Jewish life.

Doing Mitzvot Makes Jewish Values Real And Brings Greater Meaning To Bar And Bat Mitzvah

Since Judaism lacks a catechism of values, any such list is highly selective. The following list represents both ritual *mitzvot* and ethical *mitzvot.* Decades ago, the Jewish essayist, Hayim Greenberg, said, "A Jew who can name all the plants in Israel in Hebrew possesses one qualification for useful service in the State of Israel . . . but if he does not know to their deepest sounding such Hebrew expressions as *mitzvah, tzedakah, chesed, kiddush hashem . . .* he cannot carry a part in that choir that gives voice to the Jewish melody. These are the powers that build a Jewish personality." This list represents the Jewish tradition's best ways of building a Jewish personality and deepening human character.

Under each *mitzvah,* there is a list of projects that give those *mitzvot* shape and meaning. Appendix 2 lists groups and *tzedakot* (charities) that can help families fulfill many of these *mitzvot.* Some of those *mitzvot* young people can do by themselves, and others will be more appropriate for the entire family to do together. Through them, one can apply Jewish wisdom to everyday life.

Gemilut Chasadim: Acts Of Loving-kindness

So powerful is *gemilut chasadim* that the Torah begins with it: God makes garments for Adam and Eve. And, the Torah ends with it: God buries Moses. So powerful is *gemilut chasadim* that performing acts of loving-kindness is the closest that humans can come to a genuine imitation of God.

- Encourage your child to visit someone who has lost a loved one, fulfilling the *mitzvah* of *nichum aveilim* (comforting mourners.)

- Encourage your child to visit or call on someone who is ill, ful-filling the *mitzvah* of *bikur cholim* (visiting the sick).

- Encourage your child to learn games, magic, clowning, or bal-loon-animal-making skills to use in the pediatric ward of a hospital.

- Arrange to have leftover food from your bar or bat mitzvah cel-ebration taken to a soup kitchen that feeds the homeless and the hungry.

- Arrange for a food barrel to be placed in your synagogue.

- Bring leftover *chametz* (leavened food products that are forbid-den on Pesach) from your home to a local food pantry. Organize your synagogue to do it as well.

- Volunteer as a family at a soup kitchen for the homeless.

- Ask guests to bring canned food to your bar or bat mitzvah party for subsequent distribution to the homeless. A growing number of Jews are doing this *mitzvah* already.

- The debate on the Jewish acceptability of Halloween is not abating. But to ethically transform Halloween, have children collect food for the hungry rather than candy for the well-fed.

- Give three percent of the cost of your bar and bat mitzvah cele-bration to MAZON, The Jewish Hunger Fund (see Appendix 2).

- Encourage your child to write to an elected official about an important social or political issue, fulfilling the *mitzvah* of *mish-pat* (justice). Use a Jewish idea in the letter.

- Participate as a family in a clothing drive for the needy.

Tzedakah: Sacred Giving

Some Jews say *tzedakah* is the highest *mitzvah*. It is usually translated as "charity," "justice," or "giving." I prefer "sacred giving." *Tzedakah* is not what we give; it is what we *owe* as part of our covenant with God. Though many American Jews have dropped ritual practices, they cling to the practice of *tzedakah* as to a precious heirloom. Perhaps this is because Proverbs says: "Tzedakah redeems from death." It not only potentially saves individuals from a physical death. It also redeems the giver from a death of the soul.

- Choose a *tzedakah* from Appendix 2 and donate to it to honor your child becoming bar or bat mitzvah, or encourage him or her to set aside for *tzedakah* a portion of gift money. Some young people have even given away all their gift money. Several years ago, twins in California used all their gift money to help Cambodian boat people.

- Set aside some *tzedakah* every Friday night before Shabbat. Use a family *puschke,* or a *tzedakah* container. Decide as a family where the money should go. Decent, gracious, loving human beings are made, not born. This is the easiest, lowest-costing, most hands-on way of teaching the value of *tzedakah* to a child.

- Money is not the only thing that can be given. So can time. Set aside time each week for a socially redeeming purpose. Encourage your child to do the same.

Talmud Torah: The Study Of Torah

Jewish learning should extend beyond the words of the Hebrew texts. One can learn that Jewish wisdom can walk through all kinds of doors in our lives.

- Read Jewish books together as a family.
- Learn to sing Hebrew songs together as a family.
- Visit a Jewish museum as a family.

Hidur Penei Zakein: Honoring The Elderly

The elderly deserve respect regardless of their accomplishments or status. A shocking number of elderly people live in poverty. Others are part of our own families. Their stories and their lives are closely interwoven with our own.

- Your child can call, write, or visit an elderly relative or friend.
- Your child can deliver flowers to a nursing home before the start of Shabbat.

Zicharon: Memory

So precious is the *mitzvah* of memory that Torah commands us no less than 169 times to remember. Perhaps there is mystical significance in 13 being the square root of 169. At the age of thirteen, Jewish children have a fairly extensive memory, one that is both tribal and individual. They often remember Shabbat and especially remember that Jews were slaves in Egypt. Jewish parents must remember to teach their children to remember.

- Make sure your child knows his or her Hebrew name and the person for whom he or she was named. What special Jewish qualities did that person have that you hope your child would emulate?
- Find out your family's name in "the old country." Do not let it die of amnesia.
- Find out the name of the town that your family was from. Someone in your family knows this, and it is more than simply "some place in Russia." Look up the town in the *Encyclopedia Judaica* and learn something about the town and what it gave to the Jewish world.
- "You were strangers in the land of Egypt" has become "You were strangers in the land of America." Many Jews are now immigrating to this country. Most are from the former Soviet Union. Collect clothing and food for needy immigrants. Tutor immigrants in English.

Shabbat: Honoring The Sabbath

The Zionist thinker Achad Ha-Am once wrote: "More than Israel has kept the Sabbath, so has the Sabbath kept Israel." Every Jewish life should have more than a small taste of Shabbat.

- Have as many Shabbat dinners as you can in your home. Lead the family in candle lighting, *motzi, kiddush,* blessing children, and *birchat hamazon,* the blessing after the meal. Invite friends to share in your *Shabbat* celebration.

- Encourage your child to cook a traditional Shabbat or holiday dish.

- Avoid commercial transactions on Shabbat, such as business and shopping.

- Attend synagogue services as a family.

- Reserve a half-hour on Saturday to study together as a family, either from *Pirke Avot* (which is found in most prayer books), or from the Torah portion of the week.

- Tell a Jewish story on Shabbat.

- End Shabbat with *havdalah* (the service for the conclusion of Shabbat).

Kedushat Halashon: The Sanctity Of Speech

Most people assume that sanctity of speech means prayer. But sanctity of speech is much more profound. According to Joseph Telushkin, author of *Jewish Literacy,* the most violated commandment in the Torah is Leviticus 19:16: "Do not go about as a talebearer among your people."

Kedushat halashon means that we teach our children to watch their mouths just as we teach them to watch their hands, that we teach them to avoid gossip, tale-bearing, rumor-mongering, and other acts of verbal violence just as we teach them to avoid physical violence. In Hebrew, Jews call such prohibited speech *lashon hara* ("the evil tongue"). It is a negative, yet truthful statement about others. It is also called *rechilut,* which means talking about other people in a way that tends to lead to the negative.

- Urge your child to be careful about what he or she says about other people.

- Discuss a time when you or your child did not observe this Jewish value. What could you have done differently?

Kedushat Hazeman: The Holiness Of Festivals And Sacred Seasons

To be a Jew is to feel a part of Judaism's entire festival calendar. To be a Jew is to go through the cycle of the seasons as a Jew.

- Participate in a Passover Seder with your family. Ask your child to write a special reading to be used at the seder.

- Ask your child to write a prayer to use when your family lights its Chanukah menorah.

- Build a *sukkah* in your backyard. Decorate it. Have dinner, or, at least, make *motzi* and *kiddush* in it. If the weather is warm, encourage your children to sleep in it over night.

- Have the entire family attend the Purim service dressed like characters from the Megillah.

- Plant a tree in Israel each year on Tu B'Shevat, the New Year of trees.

Tzar Baalei Chayim: Non-Cruelty To Animals

Judaism teaches us to treat animals with dignity. They cannot be wantonly destroyed; animals of unequal strength cannot be yoked together; an animal collapsed under the burden of a load must be helped even if it belongs to an enemy. Judaism even addresses the psychological pain of animals and teaches that a mother bird must be sent away to spare her the pain of seeing the eggs being removed from her nest. Kosher slaughtering ensures swift, painless deaths for animals.

- Become involved with an organization that deals with animal rights.

- Give money to the local animal shelter.

- Adopt a dog or cat.

Tikkun Hanefesh: Repairing The Self

An important part of becoming bar and bat mitzvah is growing as an individual. Ancient rabbis believed that the ultimate goal of the *mitzvot* was nothing less than *letzaref haberiot,* refining the individual into better human material. Encourage children to:

- Eliminate a bad habit.

- Patch up a bad relationship by establishing shalom with another person.

- Transform a negative attitude about something into a positive attitude.

Mitzvah: The Path To Self-Esteem

One reason for doing *mitzvot* is not often articulated or understood. *Mitzvot* create a sense of human and spiritual competence in the person who does them.

Trevor Ferrell embodies the most powerful lesson I know of this basic truth. When he was about eleven years old, he helped awaken the world to the plight of the homeless. From the back of a truck in Philadelphia, he distributed blankets and hot drinks. He opened up his own shelter. He has travelled to Calcutta to meet with Mother Theresa. Trevor is a minor celebrity in the world of righteous people.

Trevor may be famous, but what is barely known about him is that he was dyslexic as a child and had to attend a special school. Trevor teaches us that the soul even more than the mind moves us to hear the Torah, in a unique way, as being personally addressed to us.

Frequently, certain learning disabilities impede a young person's ability to learn Hebrew and therefore to prepare for bar and bat mitzvah. But many children who are learning-disabled can learn Hebrew. When I work with such children, I give them as much as they can do, even if it means less Torah to read or fewer prayers to lead. This practice emerges from my conviction that bar and bat mitzvah is a status and a process. It does *not* depend on how much Hebrew you can learn.

But there is a larger question. What if a child was *incapable* of learning Hebrew? Surely this problem is not unique to our day, so let us use the collective Jewish past as guidance. If a child in a traditional Jewish society could not learn Hebrew, the community gave him a task to do. He—and it was then only *he*—would go from house to house to collect wax for candles that would burn in the synagogue. This was not a menial task. Without candles, the synagogue would be plunged into darkness. This was not only a physical darkness, but a spiritual darkness as well. When the synagogue candles were lit, the worshippers would remember the adage, *Torah or,* "Torah is Light." The child might not be able to *read* Torah, but he could help the community.

The lesson was that children owed something to the Jewish community, that there was no free ride. How do we translate that lesson to our time? I offer a radical suggestion. Children who cannot learn Hebrew often *can* learn Jewish history and culture. To them, I offer the practices of our ancestors as a model. I involve the child in a repertoire of *mitzvot* in the community, using the *mitzvot* in this chapter as a blueprint. At the bar and bat mitzvah ceremony, the child speaks about the *mitzvot* performed while preparing for truly becoming bar or bat mitzvah, for being old enough to understand the meaning of *mitzvah.*

Which mitzvot are you going to do as a family? What are the mitzvah resources in your community? Use this space as a mitzvah journal to help you plan what you will do and record your experiences.

Rites And Wrongs Of Passage

Putting The Party In Perspective

Bernie's Bar Mitzvah: *It's a show, it's food, fantasy, it's an audience participation extravaganza . . .*

Rites And Wrongs Of Passage

During a conversation on other matters, the talk suddenly turned to plans for a bar mitzvah ceremony to be held in two years. My friend heaved a massive sigh. "It's really terrible," she said, "being under this much pressure to put on a big show, to keep up with what everyone else is doing. The caterer's first question for me was, 'What theme do you want?'"

Every Jew in America has a "Can you top this?" tale about the Worst Bar Mitzvah Party of the Year. We need not list the contenders here. Someday, when the definitive volume of American Jewish Folklore is written, such fables of unmitigated ostentation will constitute a large and (almost) funny chapter.

The bar and bat mitzvah party has been much criticized over the years. And for good reason. Yet, most Jews do not know that the party is an integral part of the bar and bat mitzvah ritual. The first mention of the bar mitzvah party is in the *Shulchan Aruch* (the classic sixteenth-century code of Jewish law): "It is the religious obligation of the father to tender a festive meal in honor of his son's becoming bar mitzvah, just as he might do when the boy marries."

From a *halachic* (Jewish legal) point of view, then, the party has a proud lineage. But references to bar mitzvah parties go back even further. Scholars have a field day in locating the genuine seed of the custom.

Some say it goes back to Isaac's weaning. Genesis 21:8 says Abraham threw a feast to celebrate that event. One ancient source suggested that Isaac was weaned at the age of thirteen (Midrash, *Bereshit Rabbah* 53:10)! Therefore, the party, and, therefore, the connection to the age of thirteen.

Elsewhere, the Midrash suggests that Abraham regretted that he had rejoiced and made others rejoice at the feast for Isaac, yet did not make an offering to God. God said to him: "I know that even if I commanded you to offer your only son to Me, you would not refuse." (*Bereshit Rabbah* 55:4). This midrash teaches that the binding of Isaac was God's way of showing Abraham that he had not lost the capacity to make an offering to God.

Some say the tradition of the bar mitzvah party goes back to Rabbi Yosef in the Talmud (*Kiddushin* 31a). Rabbi Yosef was blind. In Jewish law, the blind were exempt from doing *mitzvot*. But Rabbi Yosef realized that he was already doing the *mitzvot*. Why not get "credit" for doing so? He wanted to change his status from someone who didn't have to do the *mitzvot* to someone who *had* to do the *mitzvot*.

So Rabbi Yosef made an offer. If some skilled sage could prove that a blind person had an obligation to do *mitzvot,* he would host a great celebration to mark his change in status. A little more than one thousand years later, the sixteenth-century legal authority, Rabbi Solomon Luria, drew on his knowledge of this Talmudic discussion. He reasoned that if Rabbi Yosef could celebrate that *he* was now obligated to do the *mitzvot,* shouldn't we celebrate and give thanks to God that a bar mitzvah was now obligated to fulfill the *mitzvot?* Rabbi Luria ruled that the bar mitzvah meal is a *seudat mitzvah* (a religiously commanded festive meal) on the same spiritual level as the wedding feast. The boy would have to give a religious discourse during the banquet. In Poland, the bar mitzvah discourse *(derashah)* became part of the festive meal. This was probably the origin of the bar and bat mitzvah speech, which, in the public imagination, became transformed into the famous "Today, I am a fountain pen" speech of classic Jewish comedy.

The bar mitzvah feast occurred in the afternoon as the third meal of the Sabbath. An hour before the afternoon service *(minchah),* the lad would go to the homes of his guests to invite them to the third meal. At the meal, the lad would discourse on the customs of bar mitzvah and he would lead the grace after the meal.

A Choice:
Celebration Or Conspicuous Consumption

Modern American Jews are not the first Jews to confront the ethical overtones of conspicuous consumption. Even in medieval times, there were excesses in celebration. But in the sixteenth century, Solomon Luria didn't like what he saw. In his commentary on the Talmud, he condemned bar mitzvah parties as "occasions for wild levity, just for the purpose of stuffing the gullet" *(Yam Shel Shelomo, Baba Kama, 7:37)*.

The rabbis of the Middle Ages eventually enacted laws to limit spending on festivities. They did this to protect the dignity of the less wealthy. This was identical to the original reason for a plain wooden casket at a funeral—so no one would be humiliated by having a less-than-opulent coffin. It also parallels the original reason for communal wedding rings that all brides would wear so that none would have to do without.

Beyond this, I suspect that the rabbis worried about the jealousy of gentile neighbors, who might use displays of Jewish opulence as an excuse for a pogrom. Saul ha-Levi Morteira, a leading rabbi of seventeenth-century Amsterdam (and the teacher of philosopher Baruch Spinoza), made this point in a sermon he gave around the year 1622:

> The first generation of our ancestors who left the land of Canaan knew that they were resident aliens, who had departed from their own land and come to a land not theirs. They continued to think of themselves as aliens, and they did not overreach. The Egyptians loved them and bore them no envy. But after their death, the following generation thought of Egypt as the land of their birth. They grew arrogant and became so provocative in their behavior that they aroused the envy of the Egyptians, who decreed harsh laws against them and enslaved them.

Finally, some historians suggest that these laws kept the emerging *nouveau riche* in their places so they did not threaten the status of the Jewish "old guard."

In the early decades of the twentieth century, when Jews were first becoming comfortable in America, bar mitzvah parties became especially opulent. Soon, the bar mitzvah's social component would eclipse its ritual function. The 1920s and 1930s saw the growth of the catering industry, which encouraged the transformation of bar mitzvah from a ceremony to an "affair." This era also saw the growth of gift giving in connection with bar mitzvah.

The Ethics Of Jewish Celebration

Soon, the materialism that had become attached to bar mitzvah was decried. In 1938, the noted Orthodox rabbi, H. Pereira Mendes, insisted that the bar mitzvah "not be allowed to deteriorate into merely a day for perfunctory observance or for merry-making or gifts." Twenty-six years later, the Central Conference of American Rabbis condemned the

> deterioration in the character of the bar mitzvah "affair." The extravagant consumption, the conspicuous waste, and the crudity of many of these affairs are rapidly becoming a public Jewish scandal. The lowering of standards as reflected in many bar mitzvah celebrations is in direct violation of the teaching of the Torah. The trend toward the abandonment of aesthetic standards can lead to the abandonment of ethical standards as well.

Concerns about the taste and aesthetics of bar and bat mitzvah are with us today. But there is a larger issue of the Jewish ethics of celebration. Such ethics help us understand the way that Jews view the world.

In his classic, *Paganism, Christianity, Judaism,* Max Brod taught that there were essentially three religious ways of viewing the world: paganism, Christianity, and Judaism. Christianity—particularly early Christianity—believed that man should behave as an *angel*. Reject good food, fine wine, and possessions. Enter a monastery to be ascetically sealed away from the temptations of the world. Paganism believed that man was an *animal*. Seek pleasure, good food, fine wine, and possessions. Live your life like the second reel of Fellini's *Satyricon*.

Early Christianity still has a voice in our world. We heard it in the Prohibition movement, and now in certain quarters of the anti-abortion movement. Paganism also still shapes our world. We find it in beer commercials, in *Food and Wine* magazine, in the *Playboy* ethic, in the rampant consumerism of American society.

Judaism's great contribution to the moral vocabulary of the world was that it produced a middle way between those extremes, the way of *mitzvah* and *kedushah*. God made us a little lower than the angels, but much higher than the animals. Judaism says that we neither *reject* nor *hoard* pleasure. We *sanctify* pleasure. We sanctify what we eat through *kashrut* (dietary laws), what we own through *tzedakah* (holy giving), what we drink by *kiddush* (blessing the wine), and by drinking moderately on Shabbat, on Pesach, or somewhat immoderately on Purim. We touch a drop of wine to the lips of the newborn baby. We remember the exhortation that goes with the lifted cup: *Lechayim.* Wine makes our life sweet, but should not be used to the point that it becomes addictive.

Modern Judaism (and by extension, all modern liberal religions) faces the dilemma of the split self, by which I mean: "*This* is my religious self. *That* is my non-religious self. I will let religion enter certain areas of my life. But there are many areas of my life that religion will not enter. I will not let religion enter those places because I have arbitrarily ruled that those areas are off-limits to religion."

The split self says of the bar and bat mitzvah: "The religious part of this moment is what happens in the sanctuary that morning. But then comes the closing song of the service. We say *shabbat shalom* to each other. We leave the sanctuary. We are in *profane* territory, and *profane* comes from *pro fanum,* meaning 'away from the sanctuary.' Then we can do anything we want. For a few moments, we were in the world of text, Torah, and holiness. But beyond those moments, we are back in the real world, when the lessons and Torah of the real world will be heard in all their glory."

This is not far, really, from those who say, "I don't care what the Torah says about treating your employees. When I want to hear Torah, I'll come to the synagogue. In my business, I don't want to hear Torah."

A genuine pity. More than a pity—a Jewish scandal. When I attend such affairs, I ask myself, "I *don't* want to be puritanical, but is this really about a sacred Jewish passage? Why are these children being pushed into this pseudo-adulthood of tuxedos and strapless dresses? *What are we teaching them?*"

We must remember that everything we do with our children teaches *something*. It gets taught without our even knowing it, perhaps even through osmosis. When we split ourselves between Judaism and something called the "real world," we say that we really don't take Judaism seriously, that Judaism is for dress-up occasions, that Jewish values are for public liturgy but not for private performance, that we are willfully participating in an idolatry of the self.

Toward The Middle Way: How To Sanctify Our Celebrations And Put God On The Guest List

What do we do? Putting God on the guest list means that God calls to us to conquer, in some small way, the polarities between the sacred and the profane. Early in the planning stages for a bar or bat mitzvah, it is important for parents to ask, "What Jewish values do we hope this bar or bat mitzvah celebration will embody?" Make a list of them. Your list may include compassion, dignity, justice, learning, social action, generosity, humility, moderation, a love for the Jewish people and the Jewish homeland. These are the essence of Judaism's middle way between early Christianity and ancient paganism. Plan your celebration *around* these values, and stick to them.

I know a family that asked its bar mitzvah guests to give money to UJA-Federation's Operation Exodus to help resettle Soviet Jews. I know a family that put the emblems of the twelve tribes on the tables at their son's bar mitzvah. It was their way of teaching about our roots in the land of Israel.

I know a family that feared it might be celebrating their daughter's bat mitzvah in the midst of the Persian Gulf War. The mother told me that she could not fully rejoice at the bat mitzvah under such circumstances. She took seriously the Talmud's teaching that "when the Jews are in trouble, I cannot say, 'I will go to my home, eat, drink, and be at peace with myself'" (*Taanit* 11a). She understood the midrashic teaching that God rebuked the angels for bursting into song when the Egyptians drowned in the Red Sea.

We discussed what to do and came up with the idea that she or her husband should shatter a glass at the reception right after Kiddush. Why? I had recalled that the custom of shattering a glass at a wedding ceremony probably originates with a Talmudic sage, Rav Ashi, who deliberately smashed expensive glassware at his son's wedding to reduce the hilarity and bring everyone back to reality (Talmud, *Berachot* 31a). If this is done at a wedding to bring us back to reality, then it could also be done at a bat mitzvah celebration to achieve the same purpose.

When the war ended two days before the bat mitzvah, I remembered the words of poet Monique Wittig: "There was a time when you were not a slave, remember that. You say you have lost all recollection of it, remember. Make an effort to remember. And failing that, invent." This mother was ready to invent. Her invention was an act of faith, a recognition that a ritual moment can speak to us with words we never knew possible.

I know a family that bought trees in Israel in honor of its bar mitzvah guests. I know a family that asked family members and friends to help light the candles on the bar mitzvah cake. Such a ritual is not unusual, but they chose to do it in a different way. As each guest came up to light a candle, he or she offered the bar mitzvah boy a blessing, or a word of encouragement, or a Jewish value that the young man might embody.

I know a family that put photos and biographies of Soviet Jewish refuseniks on each table at their party and asked guests to write to these captives. I know a family that put information about certain charities on each table and asked guests to contribute or learn about the causes. I know families that forego the entire culture of catering by having the party at their homes or at a summer camp.

Best yet, I know families that go to Israel in lieu of a party. They have correctly surmised that their child would soon forget the party, but a trip to Israel does not become a lost memory.

Ultimately, these are the answers: Jewish celebrations that celebrate Jewish values. The educational and spiritual part of bar and bat mitzvah can extend beyond the final hymn at the service. It can permeate the lives of our young, and it can enrich what they take with them into the world.

A friend told me that when a caterer inevitably asked, "What's the theme of your daughter's bat mitzvah going to be?" he responded, "How about Judaism?"

It's a good answer, simple yet elegant.

> *What are some of the things that you might do to "put God on the guest list" at your celebration? Write some of your ideas here.*

To A Religiously Skeptical
Jewish Parent

He drew a circle that shut me out
Heretic, rebel, a thing to flout.
But love and I had the wit to win
We drew a circle that drew him in.

—Edwin Markham, "Outwitted"

To A Religiously Skeptical Jewish Parent

There was once a time when people lived lives of faith occasionally disrupted by moments of unbelief. Today, it is somewhat the opposite. We have moments of unbelief that are sometimes interrupted—*blessedly* interrupted—by moments of faith. Traditional roads to faith seem to be incessantly blocked or hopelessly detoured.

Nowhere in Jewish life do we sense this doubt more than with the ambivalent Jewish parent. Something about the years preceding bar and bat mitzvah bring those doubts and questions to the surface.

Some parents acutely feel the social pressures for their child to "have" a bar or bat mitzvah: "Our neighbors are renting the state of Delaware for the reception, and Michael Jackson is singing, and the Prime Minister of Israel is flying in to do *motzi*."

Some parents start wondering about the meaning of Judaism and Jewish wisdom in their lives and in the lives of their children. I would even go so far as to call it *Torah-phobia*. As one father of three said to me recently about the Joseph story, a tale of sibling rivalry, "How do you make this stuff relevant, anyway?"

Some parents remember their own bar and bat mitzvah experiences with anger or boredom, or a combination of both. There is no end to the conversations that start with, "I went through this when I was a kid, and I swore that I would spare my child this dreariness."

Some parents simply become cynical about the whole enterprise, using something resembling atheism as an instrument of escape. As a parent recently said to me, "I have some real doubts about the Jewish idea of God. I've spent a long time looking at all the terrible things that have been done in the name of religion and the walls that it erects between people. It makes me wonder whether my daughter should learn this stuff and become bat mitzvah. Maybe I'm wrong to lay my stuff on her, but I can't be a hypocrite."

The Jew who sincerely struggles with the life of faith and the life of Torah is in good company. For Judaism is the only religion that has, in the words of writer Dennis Prager, "canonized its critics." Jewish literature is filled with stories about those who struggled with God: Abraham confronted God about Sodom and Gomorrah. Moses, during the incident of the golden calf, demanded that God spare the Jewish people, "or else blot my name out of Your book." Job, after losing all that was precious to him, could only listen for the voice of God that emerges "out of the whirlwind."

Elisha ben Avuya, the heretic of the second century C.E., lost his faith in God when he saw a child die while performing a *mitzvah*. His rabbinic colleagues called him *Acher* (the apostate), and yet he was never read out of our history. More recently, Elie Wiesel emerged from the Holocaust to recreate his life with the mission of forcing humanity to rethink both God and itself.

Few modern writers have come close to Anne Roiphe's achievement in the God-questioning department. In her novel *Lovingkindness,* the character Annie Johnson writes to the rabbi of the Jerusalem *yeshivah* that her daughter has joined:

> Your God asked Abraham to sacrifice his only son. Your God is always testing and teasing and placing apples in Gardens where they need not have been. He draws lines that should not be crossed and then punishes when we cross them. His tricks with waters that close over the heads of enemies are as often as not earthquakes and storms that destroy us as well or they come too late or too early. . . . I am not charmed by old stories of rabbis who meet on the streets of Vilna and tell tales of other rabbis who are so wise that they have found all but the last letter of the name of God and can show you multiples of seven that will foretell your future. The last years of our history have revealed that all the wisdom of the Talmud, all the pages of the Zohar, all the oral tradition . . . will only bring us to the ovens with our eyesight already damaged by the fine print and the dim light.

In her own life, Anne Roiphe has reclaimed the tradition she once cavalierly rejected. Many have walked similar paths and raised similar objections: religions, they say, divide people and are responsible for most of the world's evil. The Jewish idea of God, they assert, is intellectually and spiritually bogus. These Jews say they are "areligious," "nonreligious," anything but "religious." Some, certainly, greatly care about the Jewish people. Some, surely, care deeply about something called Jewish culture, though we are increasingly uncertain what that means. But believers in God, believers in the Covenant and in Jewish destiny, they are not.

Do Religions Divide People?

"Why can't people just be people?" ask those who claim that religions divide people. "Why can't there be a universal religion?"

But what would a universal religion exclude? What pearls that are peculiar to a certain tradition would go overlooked or be rejected? Think of the potential theological fender-benders such a religion would have. If you think that the world is made right by believing in Jesus, then it can't be made right by doing Torah. The two mutually exclude each other.

A generic religion is impossible because there is no such thing as a generic human being, and there won't be until the Messianic Age merges us into a great rainbow of humanity. In the interim, we all view life through the lenses of our tribes, be they ethnic, racial, or theological.

F. Forrester Church, a Unitarian minister, has put it this way:

> We all stand in the cathedral of the world. In the cathedral are a multitude of stained glass windows. We are born in one part of the cathedral, and our parents and our grandparents teach us how to see the light that shines through our window, the window that carries the story of our people. The same light shines through all the windows of the cathedral, but we interpret its story in many different ways. The light is the presence of God. And the ways we see its colors are the ways of our tribe.

There are different responses to life in the cathedral of the world. Relativists say, "All the windows are basically the same, so it doesn't matter where you stand." They may even wander from window to window. The fundamentalists say, "The light shines only through my window." And fanatics break all the windows except theirs. But the fact remains, our view of truth and reality is tempered by the way that our people view the world. The light that comes through our Jewish window is the light of Torah and of *mitzvot*. It is not the whole light. But it is our refraction of the light, and that is why it is holy.

The Messiah will show each person that the light that they have been viewing is for everyone, and that ultimately there will be one window in the cathedral of the world. Then we will have the same view of reality, one that is holy and complete. But until that day, individual peoples bask in the light that is refracted through their own particular window. Bar and bat mitzvah is the time when we bring our children to our window, point to the light, and teach them that Torah is our stained glass window.

Do Religions Create Evil?

I once heard a bar mitzvah boy trip over one of the readings in the Reform prayerbook, *Gates of Prayer:* "In a world torn by violence and *prayer.*" He meant to say: "In a world torn by violence and *pain.*" History has often taught us how effectively prayer can tear the world apart. People have killed for their gods. And people have died for their gods.

This is an age of rampant secularism. It has seen the depletion of meaning. It has seen a new idolatry of the self and of the state. The bodies that have fallen in the service of these idols litter the stage of the twentieth century like actors in a Shakespearian tragedy. More people have died at the hands of demonic anti-religious regimes, Communism and Nazism, than at the hands of all the religious leaders of history combined. The pain of the world cannot be placed only upon the altars of religion. Why not look at the strength that faith can instill, and not the pain or death it can impart?

Simon Wiesenthal, the great Nazi-hunter and a secular Jew, has said that his lack of faith goes back to Dachau. There, in that Kingdom of Darkness, he once saw a man charge people bread to use the *siddur* that he had smuggled into the camp. "If that's religion," Wiesenthal said at the time, "I don't want to be religious."

Upon later hearing that story, someone asked Wiesenthal, "You may be right. It is horrible, unthinkable, for someone to charge another person bread to use a prayer book. But what about the people who freely gave their bread away? What does it say about them, that they would trade *bread* for *prayer?*"

Bar and bat mitzvah are the time when we say to our children: "Listen, there is more than enough to be cynical about in the world. So why not learn about the sources of hope from the people who first brought the idea of hope into the world?"

The Jewish Idea Of God?

Finally, some Jews scoff that they "can't believe in the Jewish idea of God." Fine, but which God don't they believe in?

There are many gods that a Jew might *not* believe in: the highly personal God of the Bible and rabbinic literature. The God of Jewish mysticism. The God of Baruch Spinoza, the God who is inseparable from the laws of nature. The God of Martin Buber, found in an intimate relationship. Or the God of Mordecai Kaplan, who is the Power that assures individual salvation and personal enhancement.

This swift, cursory journey through Jewish thought reveals something indispensable about Jewish self-understanding—whichever vision of God a Jew rejects, he or she is in good company, since Judaism has never had a strict catechism of belief. The essence of Judaism is not the idea of God. A *midrash* (*Pesikta de-Rav Kahana* 15) imagines God saying, "Would that they deserted Me and kept My Torah." This is not explicit permission for atheism, because the rest of the verse concludes, "For when they keep My Torah, they . . . would have come back to Me." Let us not be reckless. Jewish theology must not be discarded as alien or irrelevant to the Jewish quest for meaning. But Jewish living is more powerful than being able to articulate a finely-nuanced theology. We and God find each other in those moments when we, even in the midst of overwhelming doubt, self-consciousness, and cynicism, can begin to live a Jewish life.

Bar and bat mitzvah is a time when we can truly find God—despite it all. Someone once said that there are no atheists in fox holes. I think that there are also no atheists on the *bimah* at a bar or bat mitzvah.

You May Be More Religious Than You Think

The Protestant theologian Karl Barth once said that we should never take unbelief at face value. The surprising truth is that most Jews *think* that they don't believe. Their actions belie their suspicions.

Beyond Israel Bonds, beyond fund-raising, beyond headlines about the Middle East, something about the Jewish return to Israel calls out to us in a deep and profound way. The resurrection of a people from the pits of despair reminds us of God's redeeming presence in the world. It says to us, deeply, that God does not lie. There is a purpose to history. There is hope.

The Jew who gives his or her children a Jewish education, even the parent who does so despite serious reservations and ambivalences, is saying: "I want my child to stand in the light refracted through the Jewish window. I know that my child might wander. I know that my child might become curious about other windows. But I want my child to know where home is, as well."

Consider the words of feminist Letty Cottin Pogrebin. Her children lacked even a minimal Jewish education, and therefore, were not bar or bat mitzvah. Pogrebin regrets that decision mightily:

> I did offer the children the opportunity to go to Hebrew school, but my invitation was desultory and lackluster, like a casual, "Let's have lunch one of these days"—the right thing to say, yet patently insincere. All three [children] refused my offer, contenting themselves with the vicarious pleasures of their friends' bar or bat mitzvah celebrations. . . . My children *felt* Jewish, but had little sense of being part of a historical constituency. . . . Like many of my anti-religion decisions, I have come to view this as a grievous error of judgement. Because I had a feminist axe to grind, I cheated my children out of a Jewish education and allowed them to reject a rite of tribal inclusion whose significance they were not equipped to evaluate. . . . Now in their twenties, all three of them are casualties of my rebellion. They are paying for my commitment to their pain-free non-religious childhoods with the shallowness of their ethnic foundations.

The poet Adrienne Rich once saw it this way. She speaks of the "invisible luggage of fifty years. It goes around on the airport carousel, and you wait for it, and you wonder if your luggage simply looks like everyone else's."

Our Jewish luggage is different from all others. It has been on the carousel of eternity for the last three thousand years. It is now our job, and the job of our children, to pick it up and to carry it and to make it come alive.

Which of the issues described in this chapter have been real to you? How have you confronted them? How have you dealt with them? What are some other spiritual doubts that you have encountered? Use this space to write them down.

C H A P T E R

7

The Shabbat Morning
Worship Service

Finding Your Place In The Words

I do not understand
the book in my hand.
Who will teach me to return?
Loss of custom, ruin of will,
A memory of a memory
thinner than a vein.
Who will teach us to return? . . .
We do not want to come back.
We do not know where we are.
Not knowing where we are, how can we know
where we should go?

—CYNTHIA OZICK, "IN THE SYNAGOGUE"

The Shabbat Morning Worship Service

It is the same in every Jewish congregation in North America.

Many Jews are uncomfortable with Jewish worship. Only one piece of evidence is needed to prove this assertion—the Shabbat morning bar and bat mitzvah service.

Guests arrive late, sometimes timing their arrival to their estimate of when the Torah reading will start. People don't pray. Sometimes they don't even open the prayer book. They often seem lost; they may have no idea what the service is about or what it is supposed to accomplish. They don't know what to do, where to read, what to read, what page to turn to, when to stand, when to sit, when to sing. They cannot discover the treasure in the prayer book. It is not surprising that Jews lag well behind the general population in congregational membership, in worship attendance, and in the importance they place on religion in their lives. Of all Americans, Jews have the lowest attendance at weekly religious services—about half the national average.

In too many synagogues on too many Shabbat mornings at too many bar and bat mitzvah ceremonies, there is too little participation. Jewish congregations have too often become audiences, while cantors and rabbis have become performers, masters of ceremonies, talk show hosts. People are there for *something,* but it's not the service, and it is certainly not prayer. Bar and bat mitzvah candidates were meant not only to *lead* the prayers, as a *skill,* but also to *pray,* as a *value.*

Worship—true worship—was intended to be different—to inspire, to ennoble, to induce awe. The contemporary Jewish theologian, Rabbi Eugene B. Borowitz, suggests: "The Jewish service is primarily an expression and a renewal of the Jewish people's Covenant with God. The unique feature of communal worship is sharing an experience of transcendence with other Jews as a historic community."

How is this goal to be achieved? When people pray with *kavvanah* (with sacred intention), they care about the words that they are praying. That is the meaning of the words that are written over the *bimah,* the raised platform in the synagogues: *Da lifnei mi attah omed* ("Know before Whom you stand"). When Jews pray with *kavvanah,* they know that they stand before God.

Prayer is a universal human need. Yet for many Jews, prayer is difficult. We may be estranged from the words in the very prayerbooks that we hold in our hands. We may think they are for other Jews, in other times, in other places.

But it does not have to be this way. American Jewish worship can still be transformed. We can find meaning in the poetry and the ancient words of prayer. And, if we approach prayer with the right attitude, the right knowledge, the right spirit, it may embrace us and inspire us, and, yes, it may even enlighten us.

Is The Service Theater?

When someone goes into a synagogue, it is often difficult to know how to even begin approaching the seemingly weighty task of Jewish worship. So, start by thinking of the Shabbat morning service as *theater.*

What happens at the theater? You watch a performance on a stage, complete with props, choreography, and gestures. The actors know the lines that they have learned from their scripts. The audience is passive and applauds the actors at appropriate times.

But what happens in the "theater" experience that is the Shabbat morning service? There is also a script, a script that tells a story. As in the theater, the service has its own staging, props, choreography, and script.

Take the staging, for example. Where participants in a service stand is very important. The moment when a Jewish child stands before the Ark is one of extreme sanctity. The Ark is much more than where the Torah is stored. It symbolizes the Ark in the ancient Temple, the holiest place in the world.

Take props, for example. The prayer book, in one sense, is a prop, as are the Torah scroll, wine goblets, and on Friday evening, candles.

Take the choreography. We stand at the holiest moments of the service. We bow. We bend our knees. Some worshippers even ascend onto their toes at certain points in the service.

Finally, the script. Our script is the *siddur* (the Jewish prayer book). The word *"siddur"* comes from the Hebrew word "order." The *siddur* was first compiled during the eighth and ninth centuries C.E., though the forms of the service and of many prayer texts already existed by about 200 C.E., and even earlier for others.

The *siddur* is a living, breathing, and continually changing document. That is why there are so many translations and adaptations. The *siddur* we use might be the Reform movement's *Gates of Prayer,* or the Conservative movement's Silverman *siddur,* or *Siddur Sim Shalom,* or the Reconstructionist *siddurim, Kol Haneshama* and *The Sabbath Prayerbook of the Jewish Reconstructionist Foundation.* It might be the *siddur* used in Orthodox synagogues, like Birnbaum or Art Scroll. Some of these have more Hebrew than others. Some translate the traditional texts poetically or literally. Some reinterpret theological ideas that their editors considered incorrect. Some offer greater opportunities for congregational participation than others. Some refuse to describe God as "He" or "King" or "Lord." Some are explicit about the choreography in the service—when to rise, when to be seated.

The differences between these *siddurim* are less important than what they have in common—they tell the story of what Jews hold most precious. The Jewish prayer book teaches and communicates. For centuries, it was our people's source of theology. As Rabbi Henry Slonimsky, a prominent teacher at the Jewish Institute of Religion (which merged with Hebrew Union College) once wrote: "I regard our old Jewish *siddur* as the most important single Jewish book. It is a closer record of Jewish sufferings, Jewish needs, Jewish hopes and aspirations, than the Bible itself. If you want to know what Judaism is . . . you can find out by absorbing that book."

There are also actors in the Jewish service—ourselves. We perform a sacred drama that reflects our beliefs, our needs, our dreams, our values. As liturgist Rabbi Lawrence Hoffman has noted, when the actor playing Macbeth goes home, he takes off his costume and refrains from plotting another murder. But for Jews, the parts that we play in worship are not simply roles—they are identity. "Worshippers," wrote Hoffman, "are expected to believe their liturgy even after they leave the synagogue; or, if not to believe it literally, at least to know that the story is theirs. They are to own it; it is their sacred biography."

In this sacred drama, God is omnipresent. In this sacred drama, God is talked both *about* and *to*. For God is also an actor in the service—unseen and off-stage, but present. In fact, as Hoffman notes, God even has "lines" in this "drama." We must sometimes strain to hear these lines, but they are definitely there.

The Acts Of The Script

Our script is broken into "acts," which correspond to the traditional sections of the worship service. Our script tells a story, which is the world view of the Jewish people.

Act One is the *Shema* and its blessings. In this section, beginning with the *Barechu*, the service contains words that teach us *what Jews believe*. This section condenses the core of Jewish belief. It includes prayers to the God Who creates; to the God Who shows love to the Jewish people through the gift of Torah; and to the God Who redeems the Jewish people from Egyptian bondage. The God of Act One is Creator, Revealer of Torah, and Redeemer.

Act Two is *Tefilah* ("prayer" or even "self-judgement"). It is the essence of Jewish prayer. This section is also known as the *shemoneh esreh,* the prayers of the traditional daily liturgy. It is also called the *amidah* (the "standing" prayer) because it is traditionally recited standing. *Tefilah* evokes *what we need* as Jews: to be linked to our ancestors; to believe that there is a reality that transcends the grave; to feel part of God's Holiness; to give thanks; to find fulfillment and *shalom* (peace). Little is requested of God during the Shabbat service. There are many more requests in the daily *tefilah*—pleas for healing, sustenance, forgiveness, the restoration of Jerusalem. But on Shabbat, which is a dress rehearsal for the Messianic Age, we rehearse what it will be like not to need much of anything.

Act Three is the Torah reading. It is *what we learn*. This act takes place on Mondays, Thursdays, festivals, Rosh Hodesh (the first day of the Jewish month), and of course, Shabbat. During this section of the service on Shabbat mornings, the *haftarah* is read.

Act Four is *what we hope*. It contains *Aleinu* and *Kaddish*—prayers for the ultimate universal recognition of God's unity and the coming of God's kingdom.

These are the four basic acts of the worship service. In many synagogues, especially those that are Conservative and Orthodox, there is also a prologue to the service. This consists of introductory prayers, *Birchot Hashachar* ("the morning blessings") and *Pesukei Dezimra* ("verses of song"). In Conservative and Orthodox synagogues, an additional service, *musaf,* corresponds with the additional sacrifice in the Temple and repeats some themes of the earlier liturgy. It is customarily recited after the Torah service.

Becoming Liturgically Literate

There is an old story about a convention of comedians who had been getting together for many years. Over the years, they had all heard the same jokes, so they no longer needed to tell them. They assigned every joke a specific number, and a comedian would stand up, call out the number, and people would laugh.

One comedian got up and said, "Forty-two." There was a howl of knowing laughter. "Thirty-seven." Again, guffaws. "Fifty-two." Knee-slapping all around. On a roll, he thought, he tried one more: "Ninety-seven." Nothing. No response. He sat down, dejected.

"What happened?" he asked an old crony. "That was a very funny joke. Why didn't anyone laugh?"

"You told it wrong," his friend answered.

That's the purpose of Jewish worship. The goal is to know prayers so well that they have so many associations connected with them that they barely need elucidation. They should be as familiar to the Jewish worshipper as those numbered jokes were to the comedians. Their elucidation should be as unnecessary to the worshipper as the meaning of "The Star Spangled Banner" is to the average American on the Fourth of July.

Worship can again become the way that the Jewish people passes its knowledge about itself from generation to generation. Such a task requires a common liturgical language that the praying community can share.

Here, then, are the most important Jewish prayers. The list is selective. Different Jewish movements will highlight different prayers, adding some, deleting others, changing the wording in yet others. But, in essence, these prayers form the theological underpinning of the worship experience. Each prayer has a historical meaning to Jews. But more than this—each prayer is filled with potential meaning to the Jew who is prepared to embark on a search for that meaning.

I have chosen to revive a venerable custom. In mystical prayerbooks, the margins contained *kavvanot,* meditations that prompted the worshipper to focus more clearly on the inner (and often esoteric) meaning of the prayers. I have added meditations after the explanations of each prayer. For we, in our own ways, also need *kavvanot.* We need to focus. We need to ask questions. When you go to synagogue, remember this chapter. Ask yourself the questions that accompany each prayer. Those moments of focus and questioning will help you pray. They will help you reach the heights.

Don't let this mini-encyclopedia of Jewish liturgy deceive you— Jewish worship cannot be "learned" like a vocabulary list or the multiplication tables. Knowing the meaning of the prayers out of their intended context—the worship service itself—is like knowing musical notes but never hearing them strung together to become the symphony that they were intended to be.

There is, in the final analysis, only one way to truly learn the worship service, to feel comfortable with it and to feel competent with it. You have to pray it and sing it with a congregation. Anything else is theological voyeurism, and you and your child will know it. Even if it is not explicitly required by your rabbi, I unequivocally recommend that you and your child attend services regularly during the year before (and it goes without saying, after) your child's bar or bat mitzvah ceremony.

Barchu
Praise!

בָּרְכוּ אֶת־יְיָ הַמְבֹרָךְ!

בָּרוּךְ יְיָ הַמְבֹרָךְ לְעוֹלָם וָעֶד!

Praise Adonai, the Blessed One!
Praised be Adonai, who is blessed for ever!

Barechu is the call to worship. This set of responses indicates that the formal part of the worship service is ready to begin. Formal Jewish worship requires a *minyan* of at least ten Jewish adults (in some communities, ten men).

Meditation
What distracts me and keeps me from being completely present for prayer and worship? How can I remove these distractions? What is this community with which I am ready to pray?

Yotzer*
Creator

בָּרוּךְ אַתָּה, יְיָ אֱלֹהֵינוּ, מֶלֶךְ הָעוֹלָם, יוֹצֵר אוֹר וּבוֹרֵא חֹשֶׁךְ, עֹשֶׂה שָׁלוֹם וּבוֹרֵא אֶת הַכֹּל. הַמֵּאִיר לָאָרֶץ וְלַדָּרִים עָלֶיהָ בְּרַחֲמִים, וּבְטוּבוֹ מְחַדֵּשׁ בְּכָל־יוֹם תָּמִיד מַעֲשֵׂה בְרֵאשִׁית.

מָה רַבּוּ מַעֲשֶׂיךָ, יְיָ! כֻּלָּם בְּחָכְמָה עָשִׂיתָ, מָלְאָה הָאָרֶץ קִנְיָנֶךָ. תִּתְבָּרַךְ, יְיָ אֱלֹהֵינוּ, עַל־שֶׁבַח מַעֲשֵׂה יָדֶיךָ, וְעַל־מְאוֹרֵי־אוֹר שֶׁעָשִׂיתָ: יְפָאֲרוּךָ. סֶלָה. בָּרוּךְ אַתָּה, יְיָ, יוֹצֵר הַמְּאוֹרוֹת.

Praised are You, Adonai our God, Ruler of the universe, who fashions light and creates darkness, who establishes peace and creates all things. You illumine the earth and all its inhabitants with compassion, and with goodness renew the work of creation daily.

How manifold are Your works, Adonai; You have made all of them in wisdom; Your creations fill the earth. You are praised, Adonai our God, for the splendor of the work of Your hands; and for the glowing lights that You have made, You are glorified for ever. Praised are You, Adonai, the Creator of the lights.

*This is one of several versions of this prayer.

Yotzer is the morning prayer of creation. Its theme is the creation of light and darkness. It affirms that God creates and re-creates the world every day.

The popular author, Robert Fulghum, tells the following story in his book *It Was on Fire When I Lay Down on It*. During World War II, Nazi paratroopers who had invaded Crete were attacked by peasants wielding kitchen knives and farm tools. In retaliation, the population was rounded up, executed, and buried in a mass grave. Years later, in response to the darkness of the past, Dr. Alexander Papaderos formed the Institute for Reconciliation, which is devoted to furthering human understanding. To remind himself of the meaning of life, Dr. Papaderos carries in his pocket a small, round piece of glass, no larger than a quarter. It is a piece of a mirror from a German motorcycle that as a small boy he had found shattered on the road. He used to delight in shining its reflective light into dark places where the sun would never shine, in deep holes and crevices and dark closets.

"It became a game for me to get light into the most inaccessible places I could find," he said. "I kept the little mirror and as I went about growing up, I would take it out in idle moments and continue the challenge of the game. As I grew to manhood, I came to understand that this was not just a child's game, but actually a metaphor for what I might do with my life. I came to understand that I am not the light or the source of light. But the light is there, and it will only shine in the dark places if I choose to reflect it."

Meditation

How am I making light shine into the dark places in my life? How am I separating light from darkness? How have I felt a sense of creative purpose operating in me and in the world?

Shema Yisrael
Hear, Israel!

שְׁמַע יִשְׂרָאֵל: יְיָ אֱלֹהֵינוּ, יְיָ אֶחָד!

בָּרוּךְ שֵׁם כְּבוֹד מַלְכוּתוֹ לְעוֹלָם וָעֶד!

Hear, O Israel: Adonai is our God, Adonai is one!
Blessed is the glorious realm of God for ever and ever!

It is hard to sum up the power of the Shema. The sages called it *kabbalat ol shamayim* ("the acceptance of the yoke of Heaven"). It is the central statement of Jewish faith, the realization that an eternal covenant bonds us with God. Every time we sing or recite it, we re-covenant with God and with each other. We say that we are a part of a community whose task is to bring the reality of God into the world by living ethically and by God's teachings.

The *Shema* forges us into a community that transcends time and space and circumstance. Elie Wiesel tells of a group of Jews who wanted to celebrate *Simchat Torah* in a barracks at Auschwitz. But they lacked a Torah. An old man asked a young boy, "Do you remember what you learned in *cheder*?"

"Yes, I do," replied the young boy.

"Really?" said the old man. "You really remember Shema Yisrael?"

"I remember much more," said the young boy.

"Shema Yisrael is enough," said the old man. And he lifted the boy from the ground and began dancing with him, as though he was the Torah.

"Never before," Wiesel later wrote, "had Jews celebrated *Simchat Torah* with such fervor."

That is the *Shema*'s power, and it is on our lips twice daily, morning and evening. The *Shema* has been on the lips of our martyrs. It has been on the lips of those who have sought strength. It has been on the lips of those who are about to depart from this world.

Ve-ahavta
You shall love. . .

וְאָהַבְתָּ אֵת יְיָ אֱלֹהֶיךָ בְּכָל־לְבָבְךָ וּבְכָל־נַפְשְׁךָ וּבְכָל־מְאֹדֶךָ.
וְהָיוּ הַדְּבָרִים הָאֵלֶּה, אֲשֶׁר אָנֹכִי מְצַוְּךָ הַיּוֹם, עַל־לְבָבֶךָ.
וְשִׁנַּנְתָּם לְבָנֶיךָ, וְדִבַּרְתָּ בָּם בְּשִׁבְתְּךָ בְּבֵיתֶךָ וּבְלֶכְתְּךָ
בַדֶּרֶךְ, וּבְשָׁכְבְּךָ וּבְקוּמֶךָ.

וּקְשַׁרְתָּם לְאוֹת עַל־יָדֶךָ, וְהָיוּ לְטֹטָפֹת בֵּין עֵינֶיךָ, וּכְתַבְתָּם
עַל־מְזוּזוֹת בֵּיתֶךָ, וּבִשְׁעָרֶיךָ.

לְמַעַן תִּזְכְּרוּ וַעֲשִׂיתֶם אֶת־כָּל־מִצְוֹתָי, וִהְיִיתֶם קְדֹשִׁים
לֵאלֹהֵיכֶם. אֲנִי יְיָ אֱלֹהֵיכֶם, אֲשֶׁר הוֹצֵאתִי אֶתְכֶם מֵאֶרֶץ
מִצְרַיִם לִהְיוֹת לָכֶם לֵאלֹהִים. אֲנִי יְיָ אֱלֹהֵיכֶם.

You shall love Adonai your God with all your heart, with all your soul, and with all your might. These words, which I command you this day, shall be upon your heart. Teach them faithfully to your children; speak of them in your home and on your way, when you lie down and when you rise up. Bind them as a sign upon your hand; let them be symbols before your eyes; inscribe them on the doorposts of your house, and on your gates. Thus may you remember all of My mitzvot, and do them, and so consecrate yourselves to your God. I, Adonai, am your God who led you out of Egypt to be your God; I, Adonai, am your God.

Ve-ahavta, which is part of the Shema unit, immediately follows the *Shema* in the service (as well as in Deuteronomy 6) and it is also called *kabbalat ol hamitzvot* ("the acceptance of the yoke of the mitzvot"). The *Ve-ahavta* tells us that it's not enough to know that there is a God. That knowledge must be manifest in specific actions.

What actions do we list aloud in the *Ve-ahavta*?

"Teach them to your children." Don't contract the job out to someone else. Be a living role model of the search for Jewish wisdom and Jewish values.

"Speak of them in your home and on your way, when you lie down and when you rise up." If the presence of God is to mean anything in our lives, then it must mean everything in our lives. Torah cannot only be internal. It must be external also, it must live in our homes through ritual, through *tzedakah,* through the values that we teach. It must live through the way we treat our employees, our business colleagues, even our competitors. It must live in society as a prod and a guide.

"Bind them as a sign upon your hand; let them be symbols before your eyes." These words would become the scriptural rationale for *tefilin* (the phylacteries or the leather boxes that contain words of Torah and which are worn on the forearm and on the forehead). The *tefilin* are worn during the weekday morning service. They are worn between our eyes so Torah becomes our way of seeing the world. They are worn on our arms so Torah informs our way of acting in the world. They face the heart to connote that Torah will ultimately be inside us.

"Inscribe them on the doorposts of your house and on your gates." This is the scriptural rationale for the *mezuzah* that marks the doorposts of the Jewish home. It marks the intersection between the public and the private, between the internal and the external, between us and the world.

Meditation

Can I begin to imagine what it is to love God "with all my heart"? How am I serving as a conduit of God's love? How am I bringing God into my home? Into my business? Into the world?

Geulah
Redemption

אֱמֶת וְיַצִּיב, וְאָהוּב וְחָבִיב, וְנוֹרָא וְאַדִּיר, וְטוֹב וְיָפֶה הַדָּבָר הַזֶּה עָלֵינוּ לְעוֹלָם וָעֶד. אֱמֶת, אֱלֹהֵי עוֹלָם מַלְכֵּנוּ, צוּר יַעֲקֹב מָגֵן יִשְׁעֵנוּ.

לְדֹר וָדֹר הוּא קַיָּם, וּשְׁמוֹ קַיָּם, וְכִסְאוֹ נָכוֹן, וּמַלְכוּתוֹ וֶאֱמוּנָתוֹ לָעַד קַיֶּמֶת. וּדְבָרָיו חָיִים וְקַיָּמִים, נֶאֱמָנִים וְנֶחֱמָדִים, לָעַד וּלְעוֹלְמֵי עוֹלָמִים.

מִמִּצְרַיִם גְּאַלְתָּנוּ, יְיָ אֱלֹהֵינוּ, וּמִבֵּית עֲבָדִים פְּדִיתָנוּ.

עַל־זֹאת שִׁבְּחוּ אֲהוּבִים וְרוֹמְמוּ אֵל, וְנָתְנוּ יְדִידִים זְמִירוֹת, שִׁירוֹת וְתִשְׁבָּחוֹת, בְּרָכוֹת וְהוֹדָאוֹת לַמֶּלֶךְ, אֵל חַי וְקַיָּם.

רָם וְנִשָּׂא, גָּדוֹל וְנוֹרָא, מַשְׁפִּיל גֵּאִים וּמַגְבִּיהַּ שְׁפָלִים, מוֹצִיא אֲסִירִים וּפוֹדֶה עֲנָוִים, וְעוֹזֵר דַּלִּים, וְעוֹנֶה לְעַמּוֹ בְּעֵת שַׁוְּעָם אֵלָיו.

מִי־כָמֹכָה בָּאֵלִם, יְיָ!
מִי כָּמֹכָה, נֶאְדָּר בַּקֹּדֶשׁ,
נוֹרָא תְהִלֹּת, עֹשֵׂה פֶלֶא!

שִׁירָה חֲדָשָׁה שִׁבְּחוּ גְאוּלִים לְשִׁמְךָ עַל־שְׂפַת הַיָּם. יַחַד כֻּלָּם הוֹדוּ וְהִמְלִיכוּ וְאָמְרוּ: יְיָ יִמְלֹךְ לְעוֹלָם וָעֶד.

צוּר יִשְׂרָאֵל, קוּמָה בְּעֶזְרַת יִשְׂרָאֵל. וּפְדֵה כִנְאֻמֶךָ יְהוּדָה וְיִשְׂרָאֵל. גֹּאֲלֵנוּ, יְיָ צְבָאוֹת שְׁמוֹ, קְדוֹשׁ יִשְׂרָאֵל. בָּרוּךְ אַתָּה, יְיָ, גָּאַל יִשְׂרָאֵל.

This will for ever be true and everlasting, beloved and precious, awesome, powerful, good and beautiful for us: The Eternal God truly is our Sovereign, the Rock of Jacob our protecting Shield.

You endure from generation to generation, as Your name endures; Your throne remains, as Your sovereignty and faithfulness abide for ever.

Your words live and endure, for ever a precious part of our faith, now and to all eternity.

You redeemed us from Egypt, Adonai our God, and set us free from the house of bondage.

For this Your beloved praised and exalted God; Your precious people rendered melodies, songs and praises, prayers and thanks to the Ruler, the living and eternal God.

You who are high and exalted, great and awesome, who can raise the valleys and lower the mountains, O free the captive and redeem the oppressed, and answer Your people when they cry out to You.

Who is like You among the gods, Adonai!

Who is like You, adorned with holiness, awesome in splendor, doing wonders!

Your children witnessed Your sovereignty as You parted the sea before Moses. "This is my God!" they exclaimed. "Adonai will reign for ever and ever!"

For as it has been said: "Adonai delivered Jacob, redeeming him from the hand of an overpowering aggressor." Praised are You, Adonai, the Redeemer of Israel.

The *Geulah* prayer speaks of the redemption from Egypt. It climaxes with the triumphant singing of *Mi Chamocha*: "Who is like you, among the gods, Adonai?" Moses and the Israelites sang this at the shores of the Red Sea. As we sing *Mi Chamocha*, we try to imagine walking through the parted waters of the sea. A Hasidic sect marks the last day of Pesach by pouring vats of water on the floors of its synagogue so worshippers can walk through it and relive the experience of the Red Sea. Other peoples have also tried to wade through those parted waters. They symbolize freedom and liberation, both internal and external.

Meditation

What "waters" separate me from my goals in life? When have I felt redeemed by a force more powerful than me? How have I struggled for freedom? How have I helped those seeking freedom?

Avot
Fathers or Ancestors

בָּרוּךְ אַתָּה, יְיָ אֱלֹהֵינוּ וֵאלֹהֵי אֲבוֹתֵינוּ, אֱלֹהֵי אַבְרָהָם, אֱלֹהֵי
יִצְחָק, וֵאלֹהֵי יַעֲקֹב הָאֵל הַגָּדוֹל, הַגִּבּוֹר וְהַנּוֹרָא, אֵל עֶלְיוֹן.

גּוֹמֵל חֲסָדִים טוֹבִים, וְקוֹנֵה הַכֹּל, וְזוֹכֵר חַסְדֵי אָבוֹת, וּמֵבִיא
גְאֻלָּה לִבְנֵי בְנֵיהֶם, לְמַעַן שְׁמוֹ, בְּאַהֲבָה.

מֶלֶךְ עוֹזֵר וּמוֹשִׁיעַ וּמָגֵן. בָּרוּךְ אַתָּה, יְיָ, מָגֵן אַבְרָהָם.

Praised are You, Adonai our God and God of our ancestors: God of Abraham, God of Isaac, God of Jacob; great, mighty, and awesome God, God supreme. (Some versions: Praised are You, Adonai our God and God of our ancestors: God of Abraham, God of Isaac, God of Jacob; God of Sarah, God of Rebecca, God of Rachel and God of Leah)

Grantor of love and kindness, You care for us all by remembering the devotion of our ancestors, and in love, bringing redemption to their descendants for the sake of Your name.

Our Ruler helps and saves and protects us. Praised are You, Adonai, the Protector of Abraham.

The *Avot* prayer connects us to our ancestors. They had a faith, a way of life, a way of standing resolute in the face of overwhelming odds, each with their own relationship with God.

Avot is not only about Abraham and Sarah, Isaac and Rebecca, Jacob and Rachel and Leah. It's about praying to the God of your parents and your grandparents and your great-grandparents. You are praying all the way back into history. Praying is not only speaking to God. Praying is remembering that all the generations of the Jewish people are connected to God in a covenant that does not die, but which becomes eternally reborn every time we worship as a community.

But this does not mean that we walk in lock-step with the generations. The prayer says: "God of Abraham, God of Isaac, and God of

Jacob." It does not state: "God of Abraham, Isaac, and Jacob." As Martin Buber noted, every generation must come to its own conception of God. Our way of looking at God may be different from our parents'. It may be different from our grandparents'. Yet, we are all part of the same covenantal pattern.

Meditation

What did my parents teach me? What did my grandparents teach me? What stories have they left me? What moral legacies have they left me? When do I feel their presence? What was God to them? What is God to me?

Gevurot
Powers

אַתָּה גִּבּוֹר לְעוֹלָם, אֲדֹנָי, מְחַיֵּה הַכֹּל אַתָּה, רַב לְהוֹשִׁיעַ. מְכַלְכֵּל חַיִּים בְּחֶסֶד, מְחַיֵּה הַכֹּל בְּרַחֲמִים רַבִּים. סוֹמֵךְ נוֹפְלִים, וְרוֹפֵא חוֹלִים, וּמַתִּיר אֲסוּרִים, וּמְקַיֵּם אֱמוּנָתוֹ לִישֵׁנֵי עָפָר.

מִי כָמוֹךָ בַּעַל גְּבוּרוֹת, וּמִי דּוֹמֶה לָךְ, מֶלֶךְ מֵמִית וּמְחַיֵּה וּמַצְמִיחַ יְשׁוּעָה.

וְנֶאֱמָן אַתָּה לְהַחֲיוֹת הַכֹּל. בָּרוּךְ אַתָּה, יְיָ, מְחַיֵּה הַכֹּל.

Eternal is Your power, Adonai, giving life to all [or, traditionally, "giving life to the dead"] through magnificent salvation. With faithful love, You sustain the living, and with great compassion give life to all. You support the fallen and heal the sick, free the captive and keep faith with those who sleep in the dust.

Who is like You, Master of Might, and who can compare to You, our Sovereign, who rules death and life, causing salvation to flourish!

You faithfully give life to all. Praised are You, Adonai, who gives life to all [or, traditionally, "who gives life to the dead."]

The main theme of *Gevurot* is the ultimate Messianic resurrection of the dead. Traditional versions of the prayer make that belief explicit and speak of God as *mechayeh hametim* ("the One who resurrects the dead") since traditional Jewish theology believes that God will return the dead to life in the Messianic era. The new Reconstructionist version is *mechayeh kol chai* ("Who gives life to all that lives"). Reform versions speak of God as *mechayeh hakol* ("Who gives life to all") since Reform Judaism has traditionally not accepted the notion of bodily resurrection.

"God keeps faith with those who sleep in the dust." There is something of us, something nonphysical, something nonmaterial, something beyond our bodies, that lives for ever. It's called our souls. Because we have souls, we are endowed with eternal worth and eternal hope.

In 1962, a submarine sank off the coast of Israel. All the sailors were drowned. There is a memorial to those drowned sailors in the cemetery at Mount Herzl in Jerusalem. The father of one of the sailors attended a basketball game that his son's old team won. "When my son comes back, I will tell him of your victory," he said to his son's old teammates. His son was dead, but his words were an assurance that there is a hope that transcends the grave.

Meditation
What unseen presences are with me when I pray? When have I felt the reality of my soul? When have I sensed that the human soul can transcend death?

Kedusha
Sanctification

נְקַדֵּשׁ אֶת־שִׁמְךָ בָּעוֹלָם, כְּשֵׁם שֶׁמַּקְדִּישִׁים אוֹתוֹ בִּשְׁמֵי מָרוֹם,

כַּכָּתוּב עַל־יַד נְבִיאֶךָ: וְקָרָא זֶה אֶל־זֶה וְאָמַר:

קָדוֹשׁ, קָדוֹשׁ, קָדוֹשׁ יְיָ צְבָאוֹת, מְלֹא כָל־הָאָרֶץ כְּבוֹדוֹ.

לְעֻמָּתָם בָּרוּךְ יֹאמֵרוּ:

בָּרוּךְ כְּבוֹד יְיָ מִמְּקוֹמוֹ.

וּבְדִבְרֵי קָדְשְׁךָ כָּתוּב לֵאמֹר:

יִמְלֹךְ יְיָ לְעוֹלָם, אֱלֹהַיִךְ צִיּוֹן, לְדֹר וָדֹר, הַלְלוּיָהּ.

לְדוֹר וָדוֹר נַגִּיד גָּדְלֶךָ, וּלְנֵצַח נְצָחִים קְדֻשָּׁתְךָ נַקְדִּישׁ.

וְשִׁבְחֲךָ, אֱלֹהֵינוּ, מִפִּינוּ לֹא יָמוּשׁ לְעוֹלָם וָעֶד. בָּרוּךְ אַתָּה,

יְיָ, הָאֵל הַקָּדוֹשׁ.

Let us proclaim the sanctity of Your name here on earth, just as it is proclaimed in the high heavens; as recorded by Your prophet, let us cry out one to another:

Holy, Holy, Holy is Adonai of Hosts; the fullness of the whole earth is God's glory!

We respond with blessing:

Blessed be God's seat of glory!

Following Your sacred words we say:

Adonai shall reign for ever, your God, O Zion, from generation to generation. Halleluyah!

From generation to generation we will tell of Your greatness, and to the ends of time proclaim Your holiness. Your praise, O God, shall never leave our lips. Praised are You, Adonai, the holy God.

The *Kedusha* is best known by the refrain *Kadosh kadosh kadosh Adonai Tzevaot, melo kol haaretz kevodo.* "Holy, holy, holy is the Lord of Hosts. The whole earth is full of God's glory." It is Isaiah's vision of the divine beings that surround the Divine Throne (Isaiah 6:3). And then, *Baruch kavod Adonai mimkomo* ("Blessed is the Glory of God in heaven and earth"), which was Ezekiel's response to his vision of the Celestial Chariot that carries the Divine Throne (Ezekiel 3:12). This was the most profound of Jewish mystical visions.

Those two private prophetic visions of God continue into *Yimloch Adonai le-olam, elohayich Tziyon, ledor vador, Halleluyah* ("Adonai shall rule for ever, Your God, O Zion, from generation to generation. Hallelujah!", Psalm 146:10). It triumphantly affirms that God is not just the God of the individual prophet's vision. God is the God of the entire Jewish people.

Meditation
What are those moments when I have felt exalted? What are those moments when I have felt the reality of God's Sovereignty? What are those moments when I have transcended myself and feel one with the Jewish people?

Kedushat Hayom
Sanctification of the day

Yismechu:

יִשְׂמְחוּ בְמַלְכוּתְךָ שׁוֹמְרֵי שַׁבָּת וְקוֹרְאֵי עֹנֶג. עַם מְקַדְּשֵׁי
שְׁבִיעִי כֻּלָּם יִשְׂבְּעוּ וְיִתְעַנְּגוּ מִטּוּבֶךָ. וְהַשְּׁבִיעִי רָצִיתָ בּוֹ
וְקִדַּשְׁתּוֹ. חֶמְדַּת יָמִים אוֹתוֹ קָרָאתָ זֵכֶר לְמַעֲשֵׂה בְרֵאשִׁית.

*Those who keep Shabbat and call it a delight shall rejoice in Your reign.
The nation that keeps the seventh day holy shall be delighted by Your
goodness. For you favored the seventh day and sanctified it, calling it the
most precious of days, a memory of the act of creation.*

Veshamru:

וְשָׁמְרוּ בְנֵי־יִשְׂרָאֵל אֶת הַשַּׁבָּת, לַעֲשׂוֹת אֶת־הַשַּׁבָּת לְדֹרֹתָם
בְּרִית עוֹלָם. בֵּינִי וּבֵין בְּנֵי יִשְׂרָאֵל אוֹת הִיא לְעֹלָם. כִּי שֵׁשֶׁת
יָמִים עָשָׂה יְיָ אֶת־הַשָּׁמַיִם וְאֶת־הָאָרֶץ, וּבַיּוֹם הַשְּׁבִיעִי שָׁבַת
וַיִּנָּפַשׁ.

*The people of Israel shall keep Shabbat, observing Shabbat throughout all
their generations as an eternal covenant. It is a sign between Me and the
people of Israel for ever, because in six days Adonai created the heavens
and earth, and on the seventh day ceased from work and rested.*

*Our God and God of our ancestors, favor our rest. Sanctify us with Your
commandments and let us share in Your Torah. Satisfy us with Your
goodness, gladden us with Your salvation, and purify our hearts to serve
You in truth. Adonai our God, in Your gracious love let Your holy
Sabbath be our heritage, that in it all of Israel, hallowing Your name, may
find rest. Praised are You, Adonai, who sanctifies the Sabbath.*

Kedushat Hayom sanctifies the Shabbat day, either through the
singing of *Yismechu* or *Veshamru*. We link God's holiness to the holiness of this moment in Jewish time.

Meditation

How do I sanctify time in my life? What are the holiest moments in my life? How have I made Shabbat a holy time?

Avodah
Worship

רְצֵה, יְיָ אֱלֹהֵינוּ, בְּעַמְּךָ יִשְׂרָאֵל, וּתְפִלָּתָם בְּאַהֲבָה תְקַבֵּל, וּתְהִי לְרָצוֹן תָּמִיד עֲבוֹדַת יִשְׂרָאֵל עַמֶּךָ. אֵל קָרוֹב לְכָל־ קֹרְאָיו, פְּנֵה אֶל עֲבָדֶיךָ וְחָנֵּנוּ. שְׁפוֹךְ רוּחֲךָ עָלֵינוּ, וְתֶחֱזֶינָה עֵינֵינוּ בְּשׁוּבְךָ לְצִיּוֹן בְּרַחֲמִים.

בָּרוּךְ אַתָּה, יְיָ, הַמַּחֲזִיר שְׁכִינָתוֹ לְצִיּוֹן.

Take pleasure, Adonai our God, in Your people Israel, and accept our prayer with love. May our worship always be acceptable to You. God is close to all who call; turn to Your servants and be gracious to us. Pour out Your spirit upon us, and may our eyes behold Your return to Zion in compassion. Praised are You, Adonai, Who returns the wandering in-dwelling Divine Presence to Zion.

Avodah focuses our attention on a distant part of our history—the sacrificial offerings in the ancient Temple in Jerusalem. We also remember that although we no longer have a Temple, every Jewish home is a *mikdash me-at* (a miniature sanctuary), in which the mundane can be transformed into the sacred.

My love for this prayer has little connection with any Messianic longing to rebuild the Temple and restore the sacrifices held there. I love it because of its *chatimah* (the "closing" or "sealing" of the prayer). This is my own translation: "Blessed is Adonai, who returns the wandering In-dwelling Presence to Zion." That is the prayer that I say, tears in my eyes, when I see the shore of Israel from the descending El Al jetliner. This is what I say whenever I remember that we live in an age in which Jews have come home to Israel, where, once again, we have met God. Some sages say that God's Presence was in exile with us. If that is true, then God has returned with us to Zion.

Hodaah
Thanksgiving

מוֹדִים אֲנַחְנוּ לָךְ, שָׁאַתָּה הוּא יְיָ אֱלֹהֵינוּ וֵאלֹהֵי אֲבוֹתֵינוּ
לְעוֹלָם וָעֶד. צוּר חַיֵּינוּ, מָגֵן יִשְׁעֵנוּ, אַתָּה הוּא לְדוֹר וָדוֹר.
נוֹדֶה לְךָ וּנְסַפֵּר תְּהִלָּתֶךָ, עַל־חַיֵּינוּ הַמְּסוּרִים בְּיָדֶךָ, וְעַל־
נִשְׁמוֹתֵינוּ הַפְּקוּדוֹת לָךְ, וְעַל־נִסֶּיךָ שֶׁבְּכָל־יוֹם עִמָּנוּ, וְעַל־
נִפְלְאוֹתֶיךָ וְטוֹבוֹתֶיךָ שֶׁבְּכָל־עֵת, עֶרֶב וָבֹקֶר וְצָהֳרָיִם. הַטּוֹב
כִּי־לֹא־כָלוּ רַחֲמֶיךָ, וְהַמְרַחֵם: כִּי־לֹא תַמּוּ חֲסָדֶיךָ, מֵעוֹלָם
קִוִּינוּ לָךְ.

וְעַל כֻּלָּם יִתְבָּרַךְ וְיִתְרוֹמַם שִׁמְךָ, מַלְכֵּנוּ, תָּמִיד לְעוֹלָם וָעֶד.

We acknowledge that You are Adonai our God and the God of our ancestors, for ever. You are the Rock of our life, our Protector in salvation from generation to generation. And so we thank You and sing Your praises, for our lives which are in Your hand, and for our souls, which are entrusted to You; for Your miracles which are among us daily, and for Your wondrous and great acts of every hour, morning, noon, and night. You are beneficent, for Your mercy is unending; You are merciful, for Your love is unending. You have always been our hope.

For all these things, our Ruler, may Your name be blessed and exalted, for ever and ever.

Hodaah asks us to remember to be thankful for what we have. Because it is Shabbat, there is little that we ask of God. Shabbat is a dress rehearsal of Messianic times, affording us the opportunity to imagine what life would be like without asking for anything, to have all our needs satisfied. We give thanks for all that we have, for all that we might have, for the ability to give thanks.

Birchat Shalom
The Blessing of Peace

שִׂים שָׁלוֹם, טוֹבָה וּבְרָכָה, חֵן וָחֶסֶד וְרַחֲמִים, עָלֵינוּ וְעַל־
כָּל־יִשְׂרָאֵל עַמֶּךָ.

בָּרְכֵנוּ אָבִינוּ, כֻּלָּנוּ כְּאֶחָד, בְּאוֹר פָּנֶיךָ, כִּי בְאוֹר פָּנֶיךָ נָתַתָּ
לָּנוּ, יְיָ אֱלֹהֵינוּ, תּוֹרַת חַיִּים, וְאַהֲבַת חֶסֶד, וּצְדָקָה וּבְרָכָה
וְרַחֲמִים, וְחַיִּים וְשָׁלוֹם.

וְטוֹב בְּעֵינֶיךָ לְבָרֵךְ אֶת־עַמְּךָ יִשְׂרָאֵל בְּכָל־עֵת וּבְכָל־שָׁעָה
בִּשְׁלוֹמֶךָ.

בָּרוּךְ אַתָּה, יְיָ, הַמְבָרֵךְ אֶת־עַמּוֹ יִשְׂרָאֵל בַּשָּׁלוֹם.

Grant peace, goodness and blessing, grace, love, and mercy, for us, and for all of Israel, Your people. Bless us, Loving Parent, one and all, with the light of Your presence; for by that light You gave us the law of life, and a love of kindness; justice, blessing, compassion, life and peace. May it be pleasing in your sight to bless your people Israel at all times and seasons with Your peace. Praised are You, Adonai, who blesses the people Israel with peace.

Birchat Shalom reminds us that there is one thing that we do not have—peace. It calls for an end to violence, war, and bloodshed. Some versions of the prayer ask for peace not only for the Jewish people, but for all the nations of the world as well. We remember that the accurate translation of *shalom* is not simply "peace," but "completeness," "fulfillment," and "wholeness."

Meditation
What am I doing to bring shalom into the world? Into my family? Into my life? What would give me a true sense of fulfillment and completeness?

Aleinu
It is incumbent upon us . . .

עָלֵינוּ לְשַׁבֵּחַ לַאֲדוֹן הַכּל, לָתֵת גְּדֻלָּה לְיוֹצֵר בְּרֵאשִׁית,
שֶׁלֹּא עָשָׂנוּ כְּגוֹיֵי הָאֲרָצוֹת, וְלֹא שָׂמָנוּ כְּמִשְׁפְּחוֹת הָאֲדָמָה,
שֶׁלֹּא שָׂם חֶלְקֵנוּ כָּהֶם, וְגוֹרָלֵנוּ כְּכָל-הֲמוֹנָם.

וַאֲנַחְנוּ כּוֹרְעִים וּמִשְׁתַּחֲוִים וּמוֹדִים לִפְנֵי מֶלֶךְ מַלְכֵי
הַמְּלָכִים, הַקָּדוֹשׁ בָּרוּךְ הוּא.

שֶׁהוּא נוֹטֶה שָׁמַיִם וְיוֹסֵד אָרֶץ, וּמוֹשַׁב יְקָרוֹ בַּשָּׁמַיִם מִמַּעַל
וּשְׁכִינַת עֻזּוֹ בְּגָבְהֵי מְרוֹמִים. הוּא אֱלֹהֵינוּ, אֵין עוֹד, אֱמֶת
מַלְכֵּנוּ, אֶפֶס זוּלָתוֹ, כַּכָּתוּב בְּתוֹרָתוֹ: וְיָדַעְתָּ הַיּוֹם וַהֲשֵׁבֹתָ
אֶל-לְבָבֶךָ, כִּי יְיָ הוּא הָאֱלֹהִים בַּשָּׁמַיִם מִמַּעַל וְעַל הָאָרֶץ
מִתַּחַת, אֵין עוֹד.

עַל-כֵּן נְקַוֶּה לְךָ, יְיָ אֱלֹהֵינוּ, לִרְאוֹת מְהֵרָה בְּתִפְאֶרֶת עֻזֶּךָ,
לְהַעֲבִיר גִּלּוּלִים מִן-הָאָרֶץ, וְהָאֱלִילִים כָּרוֹת יִכָּרֵתוּן,
לְתַקֵּן עוֹלָם בְּמַלְכוּת שַׁדַּי. וְכָל-בְּנֵי בָשָׂר יִקְרְאוּ בִשְׁמֶךָ,
לְהַפְנוֹת אֵלֶיךָ כָּל-רִשְׁעֵי אָרֶץ.

יַכִּירוּ וְיֵדְעוּ כָּל-יוֹשְׁבֵי תֵבֵל כִּי לְךָ תִּכְרַע כָּל-בֶּרֶךְ, תִּשָּׁבַע
כָּל-לָשׁוֹן. לְפָנֶיךָ, יְיָ אֱלֹהֵינוּ, יִכְרְעוּ וְיִפֹּלוּ, וְלִכְבוֹד שִׁמְךָ
יְקָר יִתֵּנוּ, וִיקַבְּלוּ כֻלָּם אֶת-עֹל מַלְכוּתֶךָ, וְתִמְלוֹךְ עֲלֵיהֶם
מְהֵרָה לְעוֹלָם וָעֶד.

כִּי הַמַּלְכוּת שֶׁלְּךָ הִיא, וּלְעוֹלְמֵי עַד תִּמְלוֹךְ בְּכָבוֹד,
כַּכָּתוּב בְּתוֹרָתֶךָ: יְיָ יִמְלֹךְ לְעֹלָם וָעֶד.

We must praise the Master of all, ascribing greatness to the Creator, who has distinguished us among the other nations and families of the earth by giving us a unique portion and destiny.

So we humbly bow down in acknowledgment before the supreme Ruler of rulers, the Holy One of Blessing.

God spread out the heavens and established the earth; Adonai is our God; there is none else. In truth God is our ruler, as it is written: "Know then this day and take it to heart: Adonai is God in the heavens above and on the earth below; there is none else."

Therefore we hope in You, Adonai our God, that we might see soon the glory of Your might, that the false gods will pass away from the earth, and be utterly destroyed, so that the world will be repaired in the image of Your ultimate rule. Then all flesh-and-blood will call upon Your name, for You will have turned toward You all the wicked of the earth.

All those who dwell on earth will recognize that they can bow down to You and that every tongue will pledge faithfulness to You. Before You, Adonai our God, may they bow down and give honor to Your name. May they take upon themselves the responsibility of living by Your rule, and may You rule over them forever.

For Yours is sovereignty, and in glory will You rule for ever, as it has been said in Your Torah: "On that day, Adonai will be one and God's Name will be one."

Aleinu ("It is incumbent upon us") repeats the major themes of the service: the theme of *creation* ("We must praise the Master of all, ascribing greatness to the Creator . . ."); the theme of *revelation* (". . . who has distinguished us among the other nations . . ."); and the theme of *redemption*. This is arguably the most misunderstood verse in Jewish liturgy. Some gentile rulers forbade Jews from singing it in the synagogue, believing that it insulted Christians. Actually the phrase "who has distinguished us" is not ethnic chauvinism. It means that God chose us for a unique task—to teach Torah to the world and to bring the world closer to a belief in the One God.

What are the essential elements of redemption? The Exodus from Egypt is the dress rehearsal for universal redemption. Freedom for one people—the people of Israel—must lead to freedom for all peoples. Redemption means the universal recognition that all are made in the divine image.

The second element of redemption is the weightiest—*letakein olam bemalchut shaddai,* "to repair the world in the image of God's rule." To bring the world closer to how we sense God wants it to be. Our tools for doing this are the *mitzvot.*

But there is another element to redemption—*the eradication of idolatry.* Idolatry is not only worshipping gods of wood and stone. Idolatry means treating as *ultimately important and holy* something that is *not* ultimately important and holy. The state is a god for some. Contemporary culture is a god for some. The self is a god for too many.

Universal redemption—or as it is often called, the Messianic Age—comes when humanity succeeds in eradicating idolatry. For that reason, *Aleinu* ends with the ancient hope: *Bayom hahu yiheyeh Adonai echad ushemo echad:* "On that (Messianic) day, Adonai will be one and God's Name will be one."

Meditation
How am I making God One in my life? How am I making God One in the world? How am I bringing about the day when the world will reflect the Divine Unity?

Mourners' Kaddish
Sanctification

יִתְגַּדַּל וְיִתְקַדַּשׁ שְׁמֵהּ רַבָּא בְּעָלְמָא דִּי־בְרָא כִרְעוּתֵהּ,
וְיַמְלִיךְ מַלְכוּתֵהּ בְּחַיֵּיכוֹן וּבְיוֹמֵיכוֹן וּבְחַיֵּי דְכָל־בֵּית
יִשְׂרָאֵל, בַּעֲגָלָא וּבִזְמַן קָרִיב, וְאִמְרוּ: אָמֵן.

יְהֵא שְׁמֵהּ רַבָּא מְבָרַךְ לְעָלַם וּלְעָלְמֵי עָלְמַיָּא!

יִתְבָּרַךְ וְיִשְׁתַּבַּח, וְיִתְפָּאַר וְיִתְרוֹמַם וְיִתְנַשֵּׂא, וְיִתְהַדָּר
וְיִתְעַלֶּה וְיִתְהַלָּל שְׁמֵהּ דְּקוּדְשָׁא, בְּרִיךְ הוּא, לְעֵלָּא מִן־
כָּל־בִּרְכָתָא וְשִׁירָתָא, תֻּשְׁבְּחָתָא וְנֶחֱמָתָא דַּאֲמִירָן בְּעָלְמָא,
וְאִמְרוּ: אָמֵן.

יְהֵא שְׁלָמָא רַבָּא מִן־שְׁמַיָּא וְחַיִּים עָלֵינוּ וְעַל־כָּל־יִשְׂרָאֵל
וְאִמְרוּ: אָמֵן.

עֹשֶׂה שָׁלוֹם בִּמְרוֹמָיו, הוּא יַעֲשֶׂה שָׁלוֹם עָלֵינוּ וְעַל־כָּל־
יִשְׂרָאֵל, וְאִמְרוּ: אָמֵן.

May Your great name be magnified and hallowed, in the world created according to Your will, and may Your reign be quickly established, in our own lives and our own day, and in the life of all of Israel, and let us say: Amen.

May Your great name be blessed for ever and ever!

All praise and glory, splendor, exaltation and honor, radiance and veneration and worship to the Holy One of Blessing, even beyond any earthly prayer or song, any adoration or tribute we can offer, and let us say: Amen.

May there be great peace from the heavens, and life for us and for all of Israel, as we say: Amen.

May the one who makes peace in the high heavens send peace for us and for all of Israel, as we say: Amen.

Finally, there is *Kaddish* ("sanctification"). Kaddish is in Aramaic, Hebrew's sister language. The opening words of the Christian "Lord's Prayer" were probably adopted from Kaddish.

There are several different versions of Kaddish. Often, it serves as a punctuation point between different sections of the service. But the version of the Kaddish that has most graphically captured the Jewish imagination is the use of Kaddish as a mourners' prayer.

In reality, Kaddish never mentions death. It dreams of a world when death itself has been vanquished. It is a way of saying, even against the chaos of existence and the void of mortality, that there is meaning in life. It is a fervent plea for the coming of God's rule.

I once sat at the bedside of a dying woman who had survived the Holocaust. We spoke about her life in central Europe, about her girlhood in Vienna, about the way that she met her husband. I finally asked if she was afraid of dying. She shook her head, turned to me and asked, "What lasts?"

I answered her, "Every hug, every word, every kiss, every mitzvah that you did will survive you. *'Eilu devarim she-ain lahem shiur,'* says our prayerbook: 'There are certain things that we do that cannot be measured, for though we eat their fruits in this world, they send forth a ray of light that sustains us even into the next.'"

We have ways of creating our own immortality.

Meditation
What do I have that has been left to me by someone I love? What debts do I have to pay? How do I stand upright against the winds of pain and loss?

To The Heights . . . And Beyond

The Shabbat morning service, if approached with *kavvanah*—with sacred intention and awareness and an ear toward hearing both God and hearing ourselves—can take us on a journey. That journey leads us through our fundamental beliefs and needs as Jews, to hearing the wisdom that descends from Sinai, to praying for the ultimate unity of God and the coming of God's rule.

The service is carefully and deliberately orchestrated to take us, ultimately, from the mundane planes of our lives to the heights of Sinai—and beyond.

The bar and bat mitzvah ceremony occurs within this liturgical choreography. This choreography may seem strange or esoteric or irrelevant and beyond your experience. But it is weighted with millennia of Jewish experience and wisdom and hopes. Not the least of these hopes and aspirations is that your child, who is now of the age where he or she can fully appreciate the service, will feel its full force and know, in the depths of his or her youthful soul, what it means to be a Jew who can ascend the mountain of prayers to a summit where every religiously curious Jew has climbed before.

Making The Service Your Own

Many bar and bat mitzvah families personalize the service to make it more meaningful. In fact, in many Reconstructionist synagogues, families are *expected* to compile readings and poetry to supplement and personally illuminate the liturgy. Sometimes creative readings, prayers, and poetry are added; sometimes parents will speak from their hearts to their child during the ceremony. You should consult your rabbi to find out what your synagogue's policy is in this regard. But here we walk a fine line. We want to deepen the *kavvanah* of the worship experience, but it should not so deeply reflect the personal spiritual needs of a single family that others in the worshipping congregation become onlookers to one family's pageant.

Many congregations permit—and encourage—families to create their own bar and bat mitzvah booklets for the service. With the widespread availability of word processing and desktop publishing, these booklets can be quite attractive. Such booklets include:

• A brief history of bar or bat mitzvah. If this is the first bat mitzvah in your family (a phenomenon still common in American

Jewish families), then a history of bat mitzvah is crucial here.

- A definition of *mitzvah,* including *mitzvot* that the youth did as part of the process of bar or bat mitzvah.
- An explanation of the worship service.
- The Torah and *haftarah* portions read at the bar or bat mitzvah ceremony, both in Hebrew and in its English translation. Introduce both sections with some words on their literary significance. Some people reproduce the Hebrew directly from the *tikkun,* the book that shows how the unvowelled Torah portion appears in the Torah scroll. The standard *tikkun* is *Tikkun LaKorim,* published by KTAV. The *haftarot* are found, in sequence, at the back of the *tikkun.* The English translation can come from the UAHC *Torah Commentary* or the Soncino Hertz *Chumash* (see "Go and Learn": Resources for Jewish Parents).
- Your child's *devar Torah.*
- *Tzedakot* (charities) to which you would like people to donate in honor of your child's bar or bat mitzvah.
- Personal comments from parents, grandparents, and/or siblings.

What prayers in the liturgy do you find most meaningful? What particular meanings do you associate with them? How would you turn your feelings about bar and bat mitzvah into a prayer? What would you include in a service booklet?

The Changing Jewish Family

My dear, we are living in a time of transition.

ADAM TO EVE, OVERHEARD OUTSIDE THE GARDEN OF EDEN

The Changing Jewish Family

The first literary image of the Jewish family I ever encountered was in the pages of a Jewish book that my parents gave me, Mamie Gamoran's *Hillel's Happy Holidays,* first published by the Union of American Hebrew Congregations in 1939.

Hillel's Happy Holidays was a wonderful book. It introduced us to three children: Hillel, Joseph, and Leah. Their mother shopped for *challah* on Friday afternoon. Their father came home just in time for Shabbat. They lit the candles together. They made *kiddush* together. They broke *challah* together. Life was wonderful. Life was holy.

Since those tranquil days of *Hillel's Happy Holidays,* radically different images of the Jewish family have evolved. Mother now works and might not be able to pick up the *challah.* Father comes home too late for Shabbat dinner. One parent may not even come home because of divorce. Or there may be a parent who is not Jewish, or kids who are not home for Shabbat dinner because they are doing "other things."

Our Friday night panorama of a family gathered around a table dressed with a white tablecloth as they recite *kiddush* and light Shabbat candles has given way, in many families, to fast food, pizza, or take-out Chinese in cardboard containers.

There is a spiritual crisis in many Jewish families. It is the price of many radical changes that have given us a new concept of the family and that, in the process, has given us a new concept of the role of the family in Judaism.

Our Mobility Creates Special Problems

Jews have been mobile since the book of Genesis. Abraham and Sarah started life in Ur of the Chaldees on the Persian Gulf. They then migrated north to Haran, which is in present-day Syria. Crossing the ancient Fertile Crescent, they went to Canaan (the ancient land of Israel), briefly sojourned in Egypt, and ultimately died and were buried in Hebron, back in Canaan.

Their grandson, Jacob, was no less transient. Born in the land of Israel, he fled from his brother, Esau, back to the family homestead in Haran; came back to the Land; moved to Egypt to be with his beloved son Joseph; died in Egypt; and was buried in the cave of Machpelah, in Hebron in the land of Israel.

Contemporary Jews have followed the pattern set in Genesis. Most American Jews are from "somewhere else." The new American Jewish diaspora gathers in Arizona, Florida, and California. Even in non-Sunbelt regions, Jews are moving to areas where Jews never lived before. Outside of the dwindling Jewish communities of Eastern Europe, there are few places in the world where Jews live in the same place that their grandparents did.

Our great-grandparents were often sustained by the *landsmanschaften* (mutual aid societies for immigrants). Those groups helped the needy and buried the dead. If you go into any Jewish cemetery, you will see the monuments to that period in American Jewish life, the cemetery sections originally bought by these burial societies, painstakingly maintained over the years by networks of cousins' clubs.

Times have changed. Our children will not know what it means to be part of a burial circle or of a cousins' club. Who will inherit the responsibility of maintaining graves so that the family will come to visit and remember? Will the task fall to a son who now lives in Atlanta and a daughter who moved to Los Angeles and a cousin who wound up in Butte, Montana?

The extended family is on the ropes. Many Jews were nourished by memories of Passover seders and breaking Yom Kippur fasts around a large table at an aunt's house. That aunt now lives in West Palm Beach; one cousin lives in South Bend, Indiana; one child lives in Houston, another in Boston. Once upon a time, transportation to a seder was on foot. Then, it was a subway ride away. Then, a car ride away. It now entails Frequent Flyer mileage.

Family mobility leads to increased distances between the generations. A doll is now being sold of an old man with white hair and a white beard. It wears a *yarmulke* and *talit*. The doll is called Grandpa Binyamin. It exists because our children don't have real, live, in-the-flesh Grandpa Binyamins anymore. *Bubbe* and *zeyde* once lived in our homes. Living with a grandparent was often an enriching human and Jewish experience. Grandparents are second *only* to parents in the transmission of values. What happens to Judaism when contact between the generations withers? It, too, can wither and atrophy, and become a lost and amorphous vestige of another era and another time.

Divorce

The divorce rate in the United States may be as high as fifty percent. One-eighth of currently married Jews have been married before. Studies show that of all ethnic groups, Jews are *most* likely after a divorce to remarry. Most do so only once, but increasing numbers of American Jews are now on their third marriages. Remarriage creates a whole new constellation of people in a family's life, a constellation that, to me, is most poignant whenever I orchestrate the delicate choreography at a bar or bat mitzvah ceremony, when I have to calculate how to give *aliyot* to four sets of grandparents, some of whom are themselves divorced and remarried.

Psychotherapist-rabbi Edwin Friedman believes that the actual rite of passage is never *only* the ceremony. The passage takes place throughout the entire year that surrounds the actual celebration. All family relationships seem to go into a state of flux during this period.

Because Jews have a very heavy investment in their children's "performance," there is more parental tension during bar and bat mitzvah than at any other significant moment in the Jewish life cycle. Bar and bat mitzvah parents also must face the expectations of their own parents and families, both for their children and for themselves.

When parents are separated or divorced, this tension gets heightened. Who sits where? Who gets which honor? Who won't stand next to whom? Should the new spouse or girlfriend or boyfriend have an honor? Should there be one party or two? If there are two, which party should the child go to? This can all get very distasteful, especially if the husband or wife "gets custody" of the synagogue, along with remnants of the old network of friends.

Most rabbis can resort to their synagogue's rules about who gets honors. But this doesn't really solve anything, for the rabbi is frankly powerless to "solve" it. It is the responsibility of the divorced and separated parties to work it out.

Rabbis try very hard not to get caught between warring family factions. They establish an implicit (or even, explicit) rule that no one should get hurt at a bar or bat mitzvah, that everyone's dignity and feelings will be respected. Rabbis will remind families that their battles should not eclipse the real focus, which is the bar and bat mitzvah of their beloved son or daughter, grandson or granddaughter.

Rabbis try very hard to put the responsibility squarely where it belongs. Years ago, in my first congregation, a couple was involved in a divorce case that had become a local scandal. Their son's bar mitzvah ceremony was approaching. The war drums were beating, and I, the rabbi, was in the middle. There was fighting, bickering, yelling: "You can't have an *aliyah!*" "I don't want your parents coming up!"

I finally sat down with them. "You have a choice," I told them, "and the deadline is rapidly approaching for you to make that choice. The choice has nothing to do with who gets which *aliyah.* You can choose how your son will remember his bar mitzvah day. He can remember that your arguing tore his day apart. That traumatic memory will last forever. Or, he can remember that the two of you loved him more than you disliked each other. You choose."

They chose correctly. They asked me to construct the service to avoid any difficulty. I divided the *aliyot* so that the estranged parents were on the *bimah* at different times. Our synagogue's usual custom was to call up all the grandparents together for a group *aliyah;* instead, they came up in separate pairs. Though it was my usual practice to include the entire family in a circle before the open Ark as a final blessing, in the interests of *shalom* I omitted that custom, instead blessing the child alone. It worked out smoothly. Few people knew that we had reshaped our usual synagogue traditions for that particular ceremony. The day went without incident. We all breathed a massive sigh of relief.

In general, then, a basic rule for bar and bat mitzvah etiquette when there has been a separation or divorce: Cool it. Declare a truce.

Don't pull your child apart emotionally. And more than anything else, prove to your child that you love him or her *more* than you now dislike (or distrust or no longer love) each other.

Thawing Out The Family Ice Floes

Some families simply don't get along. There are long-standing feuds between members of families that go back to Vilna in the last century. Many of the same issues that surround divorce and separation also emanate from this general family discord.

When Edwin Friedman looked at the entire phenomenon of bar and bat mitzvah, he began to understand the pressures that Christians feel around Christmas time. They may become extremely anxious. They may shop for gifts beyond their means. Drinking may become more frequent.

Life cycle ceremonies are stress points in a family's life. And yet, they can also refocus and heal the family.

I remember how one mother in my congregation was anxious about her son's upcoming bar mitzvah day. She had remarried after divorcing her first husband (the boy's father), who had then died. Her former in-laws had never reconciled themselves to their son's early death. All the family problems that had been submerged over the years were surfacing in the weeks before the bar mitzvah ceremony. "Surfacing" is the wrong word; "exploding" is much closer. The woman's former in-laws were verbally abusive to her, making her life absolutely miserable. When they came up for their *aliyah* at the bar mitzvah, they were virtually paralyzed by their tears. The image of their deceased son in the very visible form of their grandson standing next to them was overwhelming for them. The whole experience was a nightmare for everyone involved.

Months later I was speaking to the woman on the phone. "Oh by the way," she said, "you remember my former in-laws, don't you?"

"Yes," I replied tentatively.

"Well, they're over and they send regards."

"They're over at your house? What happened?"

"I don't really know," she said. "But ever since the bar mitzvah, things have been just fine. I decided that I would use the bar mitzvah experience to reshape things. I had the choice of allowing them to continue this 'stuff,' or moving on to a different level."

Family dynamics are like ice floes. At a significant life-cycle moment, they can thaw out and then solidify in a different configuration. Sometimes a bar or bat mitzvah can successfully break up the emotional ice floes and help create new and more healthy ways of being a family.

Jews And Non-Jews: Yours, Mine, And Ours

Nationally, the intermarriage rate is as high as fifty percent. In some places, it nears seventy percent. It is a phenomenon that is here to stay. Add to this the increasing numbers of converts to Judaism in the Jewish community, and you can well imagine the challenge of a bar or bat mitzvah ceremony when there are significant numbers of non-Jewish family members attending. (See Appendix 1 for suggestions on what to tell non-Jews who come to a bar or bat mitzvah).

The answer to the questions that emerge about intermarriage and the bar or bat mitzvah will largely depend on the branch of Judaism with which you are affiliated.

Orthodox and Conservative Judaism state that the child of a mixed marriage is Jewish only if the mother is Jewish, or if the child has been converted to Judaism according to Jewish law at birth or shortly after birth.

For many years, Reform Judaism has stated that a child is considered Jewish if either of its parents is a Jew and if the child has been raised and educated as a Jew. The Central Conference of American Rabbis reaffirmed this practice in 1983 with its statement on patrilineal descent. Likewise, the Federation of Reconstructionist Congregations and Havurot first officially endorsed the idea of patrilineal descent in 1976.

The bar or bat mitzvah ceremony of a child of intermarriage is a powerful moment. As Susan Weidman Schneider said in her book, *Intermarriage: The Challenge of Living with Differences Between Jews and*

Christians: "After birth, there are few other ceremonial occasions that provide opportunities for the interfaith couple to express how they're raising their children and what their goals are for them." Sociologist Egon Mayer notes that "bar mitzvah has emerged as the signal Jewish ceremony by which an intermarried family publicly proclaims that their child is being raised as a Jew."

Children Of Converts

For the child of a marriage in which a conversion has occurred, bar and bat mitzvah also has great power. The parent who converted to Judaism may consider the bar or bat mitzvah a validation of his or her choice of Judaism. The bar and bat mitzvah celebrates the family's Jewish identity. This is true for all Jews, to be sure, but even more so for a conversionary family.

A woman in my last congregation converted to Judaism eighteen years after marriage and a year before her daughter was to become bat mitzvah. "My children," she once told me, "are able to experience their Jewish lives in the right sequence. I haven't done that. After all, my children helped me pick out my Hebrew name!" She continued:

> My daughter's bat mitzvah proved that my joining the Jewish people wasn't just something going on in my head. It was real. Rebecca is the first woman on my side of the family to become bat mitzvah. But she was also the first woman to become bat mitzvah in *my husband's* family as well. Although I didn't have to prove anything to my in-laws, it was nice to be able to do so. The sad thing is, my children may also be the *only* children to become bat or bar mitzvah in my husband's family in this generation.

What Can A Non-Jew Do In The Service?

All movements in American Judaism try to be as welcoming as possible within their own ideological frameworks. Still, the extent of a non-Jewish relative's involvement will depend upon the movement of Judaism with which you are affiliated. The synagogues within a movement are not monolithic; each has its own standards, and some of these standards are open to debate and revision.

Many Orthodox congregations in the United States do not let intermarried families become members. Conservative Judaism welcomes intermarried families who are living their lives within a Jewish context. Both Reform and Reconstructionist movements officially encourage their congregations to welcome the intermarried, supporting efforts to include intermarried families in synagogue life and to educate the children of intermarriage. It is left to the judgement of the individual synagogue how to best fulfill the mandate of outreach.

How would such positions influence a non-Jewish parent's participation at a child's bar or bat mitzvah ceremony?

In Orthodox and Conservative synagogues, a non-Jewish parent would not ascend the *bimah* to say the blessings over the Torah. But beyond this prohibition, some Conservative synagogues allow the non-Jewish parent to come up to the *bimah* when the bar or bat mitzvah is being blessed, to stand in place for the *shehecheyanu,* or to say a personal prayer on the *bimah.* Some encourage the non-Jewish parent to publicly reflect on the bar and bat mitzvah experience at the reception.

Reconstructionist synagogues have a variety of attitudes towards the participation of non-Jews in synagogue ritual. The nature of participation is often similar to Reform synagogues, though most Reconstructionist synagogues do not permit non-Jews to say the blessings over the Torah.

As one might expect in a movement as pluralistic and diverse as Reform, there is a wide variety of opinion on the matter of non-Jewish participation in the liturgy.

Most Reform synagogues believe that it is inappropriate for a non-Jewish spouse to lead the major segments of the service, to publicly recite blessings, or to utter phrases like *asher kideshanu* ("Who has commanded us") or *asher bachar banu* ("Who has chosen us"). Such phrases are in the Torah blessings and in the candle blessings, blessings usually performed by parents in connection with a bar or bat mitzvah. There are theological reasons for this decision, since God did not command non-Jews to perform such ritual *mitzvot* nor did God choose them by giving them the Torah.

Some Reform congregations permit a non-Jewish relative to publicly recite a personal prayer or share his or her feelings related to the bar or bat mitzvah ceremony. Some believe that their participation should be limited to specific psalms or responsive readings, preliminary prayers before the "formal" service begins (before *Barechu),* or special prayers that are not found in the regular liturgy, such as the *shehecheyanu,* thanking God for "keeping us alive, and sustaining us, and allowing us to reach this season."

According to a study completed in 1991, a significant minority of Reform congregations let non-Jewish parents perform certain ritual acts connected to bar and bat mitzvah. The rationale is that the non-Jewish parent's decision to raise the child as a Jew deserves to be honored and recognized by the congregation. Some congregations let non-Jewish mothers light and bless Shabbat candles. They may let non-Jewish parents say the blessing over the Torah, hand the Torah to their child, or open the doors of the Ark during the Torah service. They may let a non-Jew stand as a silent witness next to his or her spouse during the reading of the Torah blessing. Some congregations, believing that the Hebrew Bible is the common spiritual inheritance of all who accept its message, let non-Jewish parents or grandparents read the English translation of the Torah or the *haftarah* portion.

A New Blessing For Non-Jewish Parents

The problem of gentile participation in a bar or bat mitzvah ceremony illustrates a classic Jewish tension. We want to affirm the infinite worth of each individual. We want parents who have nurtured a Jewish child to publicly express their love and their devotion to the God whom we share. On the other hand, when we publicly pray, we want our prayers to have a Jewish legitimacy and authenticity.

I have sought to solve this dilemma in the following way. I understand the liturgical climax of the bar and bat mitzvah ceremony to be the Torah reading. Those words have the highest sanctity of any recited during a service. They also symbolize the Jewish people's unique covenantal relationship with God. Therefore, I cannot ask a non-Jewish parent to say *asher bachar banu* ("who has chosen us") while reciting the blessing over the Torah.

But consider how many non-Jewish parents have supported their child's Jewish education. I think of two old friends in my last congregation. The father is Jewish; the mother, who is from a Midwestern

Methodist background, is very sympathetic to Judaism. No longer a practicing Christian, she has not converted to Judaism because she fears this would hurt her parents. Years ago, she participated in an Introduction to Judaism class that I offered at our synagogue. At the last class, everyone offered a concluding statement. Her reflection was: "I came into this class mostly to learn about the Jewish past. I leave this class understanding my family's Jewish future."

This couple's family is filled with Jewish commitments. The father is active in the synagogue, and was president of the Men's Club and chairman of the Adult Education Committee, and has become a rather learned Jew.

How did they communicate their family's religious identity to their two daughters? "We taught them that I am Jewish, and Mom is not," the father once said. "We are a Jewish family. We only have Jewish symbols in our home. We only have Jewish celebrations in our home. We are part of the Jewish community. We have thrown our lot in with the Jewish people."

My wife and I recently sent their daughter a bat mitzvah gift. She has no doubts about who she is. And that is as much her non-Jewish mother's doing as it is her father's.

There are many non-Jewish parents like this one. They enthusiastically support their children's Jewish education and upbringing. They should be honored. And so, I created the following prayer, which I invite the non-Jewish parent to read after the Jewish parent has given thanks in Hebrew for the gift of Torah:

O God of all humanity:

We lift our voices in gratitude that the Torah has come into the world through the Jewish people.

We lift our voices in gratitude for the ideals it teaches: justice; compassion; devotion; the partnership of mind, heart, and deed.

We lift our voices in gratitude that our son/daughter today takes his/her place among the people of Israel. We pray that he/she will do so with pride and joy. As You called Israel to be a light to the nations, so, too, we pray that our son/daughter will be his/her own ray of light to the world.

The message of the blessing is very clear: "I am proud that my child is a Jew. I am proud that the Torah that he or she reads today is part of the spiritual inheritance of the entire world. I am grateful to have been part of that process."

In all non-Orthodox movements, the issue of non-Jewish participation in the worship service is under constant discussion. Such discussion is yet another example of the dynamic changes that Judaism must confront. In all cases, if your family situation involves intermarriage, discuss your synagogue's customs with your rabbi. It is an area of great concern and sensitivity, and each rabbi treats it as such.

Dealing With Non-Jews' Sensitivities About Bar And Bat Mitzvah

Ideally, non-Jewish members of the extended family support (or, at least, are neutral about) your raising your son or daughter as a Jew. But this is not always the case. Beyond the issue of participation in the service, there may be other issues related to intermarriage that surface in connection with bar and bat mitzvah.

A Jewish woman in my congregation told me about her non-Jewish mother-in-law: "My daughter's bat mitzvah ceremony is coming up. My husband, as you know, is not Jewish. But he wants our girl to be Jewish and to get a Jewish education. His mother is another story. We invited her to the ceremony, and frankly, I don't know if she'll come. I guess that she's always been angry that her granddaughter wasn't baptized and that she's not being raised as a Catholic. I don't know what to do."

Just as there are sacred moments in Jewish time, from *berit milah* or baby-naming to bar and bat mitzvah to confirmation and beyond, Christianity also has its own sacred moments: baptism, first communion, confirmation, and beyond. We can well imagine a non-Jewish grandparent's pain when a grandchild is not baptized. Such pain might not be anti-semitism. It may simply reflect a great love of the Christian tradition and of a family's tradition. It may even be something as deep as a fear for the fate of their grandchild's soul within the context of their religious beliefs.

For years, how that grandchild is being raised religiously somehow winds up on the back burner. It may surface from time to time, usually during the winter holidays and perhaps at Easter and Passover. But then bar or bat mitzvah comes, and the grandparents confront the issue again. This time it seems irrevocable. There is no question—their grandchild is a Jew.

What can parents do about these feelings from other members of the family?

- Any bigotry in their comments should not be tolerated. When a family member expresses such sentiments, they should be dealt with firmly and lovingly: "You know, Dad, I'm really surprised to hear you talk that way about the Judaism of my household. You always raised us to be so much more tolerant than that."

- Be extremely clear with your non-Jewish loved ones. Such clarity about the religious identity of your family hopefully started when you got married. You must be able to say, "Our family is Jewish, and our children are Jewish. We never intended to hurt you. We would love to share our joys with you, to the extent that this is possible. But we know that we will always love you, and we know that our son (or daughter) will always deeply love you, also."

- Give them a copy of Appendix 1 in this book, which is designed for non-Jewish guests.

Sometimes anger from non-Jewish family members is not really anger. It is fear—fear of a cultural difference that will "assault" them at the bar or bat mitzvah ceremony and celebration.

You can honor your extended family's ethnicity during the post-ceremony party by selecting music and/or serving food of their ethnic group. Such relatively small gestures can celebrate your family's diversity. It can even help create a bit of *shalom*.

In June, 1983, *The New York Times* wrote about a "bar mitzvah with a Vietnamese flavor." Paul Steinman's mother, Jo, was originally a Buddhist named Ngoc Suong Tu. She met Ron Steinman, an executive with NBC News, in Vietnam, fell in love, and converted to Judaism. Over the years, Jo and Ron raised three Jewish children. Jo was active in our synagogue's Sisterhood. Her magisterial cooking of traditional Vietnamese dishes earned her a richly deserved reputation.

Those dishes were served at Paul's bar mitzvah party. The Steinmans rejected a catered event for a big home-cooked meal. Jo's mother, Ba Thi Tu, helped with the cooking for days. Missing from the menu was stuffed derma, matzah ball soup, and chopped liver. Instead, and to no one's disappointment, was veal with black mushroom sauce, Vietnamese meatballs, beef chow fun, chicken and cashew nuts, rice noodles.

Two distinct cultures created a celebration that touched everyone deeply. "It was a desire to put on a party in one's own image," Jo told the *Times*. "That became particularly important with the kind of family we have. After all, there aren't many Vietnamese Jewish families."

The Steinmans wanted to create a party consonant with their self-image of a family fed by two ethnic streams, but that now had one religious identity.

Years later, Jo's daughter, Linda, became bat mitzvah. On the pulpit, I spoke about the twin streams that had created her, Jewish and Vietnamese. I reminded her of the plight of the Vietnamese boat people, a cause in which her family had been particularly involved. I reminded her that she was descended from two peoples who had helped shape the moral map of the world in our century. And she understood.

In the interests of *shalom,* says the Talmud, there are certain things that we do for non-Jews as well as Jews. *Shalom* here does not mean "expediency." It does not even mean "keeping the peace." It means something greater. It means moving the entire cosmos to a higher level.

If you have non-Jewish family members, what can you do to make them more comfortable? How can you help them be involved and participate?

C H A P T E R

9

After The "Thank You" Notes
Helping Your Jewish Teenager Develop
Jewish Values

Let young people . . . be sure that every deed counts, that every word has power, and that we all can do our share to redeem the world in spite of all its absurdities and frustrations and disappointments. . . . Let them remember to build a life as if it were a work of art.

ABRAHAM JOSHUA HESCHEL, ABC INTERVIEW, 1972

After The Thank You Notes

I was once talking to a father and son on the eve of the boy's bar mitzvah ceremony. The boy was very well prepared. At a certain point in the conversation, the father sent his son out to the car. He then asked if he could say something to me. I had no idea what to expect.

"I guess you could say, Rabbi," he said, "that this day's been coming for a long time. Frankly, all I want for my son is what happened for me. Almost thirty years ago, I was bar mitzvah in a synagogue near here. I was a pretty shy kid, and I was really scared that I wasn't going to make it. I pulled it off. Ever since that day, when I went back to junior high school, when I went into high school after that, I *knew*. I knew that I could do something and prepare for it and it would be all right. I only hope that Paul has that. That's all I wanted to say."

The boy did fine at his bar mitzvah ceremony. But the father was articulating something deeper and more profound than parental apprehension. He was saying that bar and bat mitzvah is more than a spiritual achievement. It is a moment of passage, a moment that can have an important effect on a young person who is just coming into his own.

What kind of passage can it be for a young person? In his classic work *Childhood and Society,* psychoanalyst Erik Erikson explained that each person goes through eight distinct psycho-social stages. Each stage represents certain inherent tensions in the human personality and each tension must be resolved if the individual is to enter the next stage of life.

What would Erikson say about bar and bat mitzvah, which represents the passage from school age to adolescence? If young people are too focused on the *skill* of becoming bar and bat mitzvah, if they focus only on performing competently on the *bima,* then Erikson would relate this to the crisis of every school-age child, to the latent fear in every young child's heart: *"I hope I don't screw this up!"*

Pastoral psychologist Donald Capps says this concern for competence carries its own perils. He has warned that the ritual passage into adolescence can be too formal and too perfectionistic. By equating technique with truth and sacrificing all other values to proficiency, he said, all that remains is empty ceremonialism.

As young people approach bar and bat mitzvah, I tell them (in the presence of their parents), "Please don't hear this as permission to slack off in your Hebrew preparation. If I had the choice between a kid who knows everything cold, but has no real feeling for what it means to become bat mitzvah, or the kid who has really come to love the synagogue, doing *mitzvot,* and Jewish learning, but occasionally makes some mistakes in Hebrew, I would prefer the second kid." To parents, I say, "Don't let the rite get in the way of the passage."

Now that the ceremony is over, now that the photocopied sheets of Torah and *haftarah* are buried somewhere beneath the basketball magazines, now that the "thank you" notes are finally written—what now? Where is the true depth of the Jewish passage from childhood to adolescence? Our tradition provides an answer. Let us return to the textual sources of bar and bat mitzvah and to the pages of the Midrash. Let us examine the tasks of adolescence that emerge from its pages.

Task Number 1: Shattering The Idols

It may be the most famous Jewish story in the world that is *not* in the Torah. Abraham's father, Terach, sells idols in Ur. He goes away on business, and leaves his young son, Abram, whose name will be changed to Abraham, in charge. Abram shatters all the idols in the store with a stick, and he places the stick in the hand of the largest idol. When Terach returns, he looks at his ruined merchandise and demands, "What happened?"

"Oh, father," Abram says, "the small idols got hungry and they started fighting for food. Finally, the large idol got angry and he broke them into little pieces. It was terrible. I don't want to talk about it."

"Wait a second," says Terach. "Who are you kidding? Idols don't get hungry. They don't get angry. They don't speak . . . they're just idols."

Smiling, Abram says, "So why do you worship them?" With that, Abraham made his break with idolatry, and discovered monotheism.

Abraham shattered the idols of his father when he was thirteen years old. Abraham is us. That tale is an essential part of our people's memory. It is the way we define ourselves. We are the children of an iconoclast.

Which idols should our post-bar or bat mitzvah child smash?

The Idolatry Of The Fast Track

I knew where this conversation was going even as it began. "Rabbi," the mother of the soon-to-be confirmand was saying, "about that essay that my son has to write for confirmation. Does he really have to do it? When you consider the baseball team, and the SAT class, and the honors program. . . ."

I asked the agitated mother, "Why not just get off the merry-go-round? Why not reject all the pressure and the competition?"

"I can't," she answered. "This is the real world. My kid needs all this to get into a good college."

The pressure on our kids to rack up achievement points mounts yearly. It is forcing them to sacrifice their Jewish involvement on the ephemeral altars of competition.

Parents, too, get caught up in this relentless American religion of college admissions. Princeton, the headquarters of the Educational Testing Service, has replaced Jerusalem as the Holy City. Our young people are taking the SATs earlier and earlier.

Yet, the fast track *does* let us insert Judaism into the equation, although parents and children often forget that. Colleges seek well-rounded students who have values and commitments. It's not just academics and traditional extracurriculars like school sports, the debating team, or playing the flute. Being involved in synagogue youth groups indicates that a teenager cares about higher values. It shows an awareness of the larger society. It shows that the student has gone beyond the self.

The Idolatry Of Achievement

Rabbi Harold Schulweis of Encino, California, has summed up the moral crisis of childhood this way:

> The Jewish child learns about good and bad from Jewish parents and how they value him. In the sentence, "Larry is a good boy," "good" does not refer to spontaneity, to gentility, to compassion, to altruism. "Good" means the child's ability to bring home the extrinsic marks of success, and "bad" means bringing home an F. Goodness is unrelated to the notion of *mitzvah,* to sensitivity to the concerns of other people.

We Jews learned, centuries ago, that our lives have inordinate meaning. The meaning of life is not necessarily achievement. It is to be holy, to be a member of a holy people. There is an obituary in my files for a wonderful young man, Ivan (Yitzchak) Tillem. In 1989, he died in a plane crash with congressman Mickey Leland. He had been flying to Ethiopia to help Ethiopian Jews. Tillem was a strikingly handsome Orthodox Jew. He died the day before his thirty-third birthday. An orphan, he had graduated from Cardozo Law School, became an investment banker, and was a millionaire before he was thirty.

Ivan Tillem had nothing, he had it all, and he gave it all back. Ivan Tillem used his fortune to help save the world. He was a major giver to Ohel, a Jewish orphanage in Brooklyn, because, in true Jewish fashion, he remembered his roots. Ivan Tillem never forgot the sound of the rattle of the coin in the bottom of the *puschke.* He lived his life on the fast track, amassing a vast personal fortune. His life teaches us the lesson: be successful, but remember from whence you have come.

Task Number 2: Building Sanctuaries

According to the Talmud, Bezalel was thirteen when he built the Tabernacle, the portable sanctuary that our ancestors carried through the wilderness to house the tablets of the Ten Commandments and to be their central place of worship.

Our teenagers can also be Bezalels. With the help of their parents, they can build sanctuaries out of Jewish values. Like the first sanctuary, those contemporary sanctuaries will be portable. But unlike the first sanctuary, these sanctuaries can last all their lives.

The Sanctuary Of Jewish Memory

The first sanctuary that might be built in the years after bar or bat mitzvah is one that has been under construction all along. Memory is the fundamental commandment of Jewish life. It defines who we are, linking our past to our present and teaching us how to create the future.

The spiritual life of the family begins when we reclaim our past. If we have forgotten our children's Hebrew names, we must try to remember them. If we have forgotten our parents' Hebrew names, we must try to remember them. If we have forgotten the holy qualities of the great-aunts and uncles for whom our children were named and for whom we were named, we must try to remember them. If we have forgotten the names of the cities in Europe where our families are from and the names of their great teachers, we must try to remember them.

I will always remember something that happened to me at the Jewish Museum in New York many years ago. Walking through an exhibit of Czech Judaica that the Nazis had intended to be a permanent record of a dead people, I found myself gazing at a Torah curtain that had once hung over the Holy Ark in the Altneuschul in Prague, the oldest synagogue in Europe. The curtain was from 1608. It was the oldest Torah curtain in Europe. Then I read the name of the person who had given that Torah curtain to the Altneuschul more than three centuries ago—Natan Bar Yissachar, also known as Karpel Zaks. As I saw that name, my eyes filled with tears and my hands began to shake, for a branch of my mother's family was from Prague, and her maiden name was Karpel.

But do not think that if you lack an early seventeenth-century Torah curtain from Prague that you lack access to Jewish memory. Each of us is a descendant, and each of us is also an ancestor. Our task is not only to inherit memory, but also to *create* memory. Before you and your child jointly decide that his or her Jewish education has ended, ask your child: "Do you know enough to create Jewish memories for your own children? Do you know enough to run the Seder when Grandpa and Grandma and Daddy and I are gone? Do you know how to teach your children the story of chanukkah? Do you know how to say Kaddish? Do you have some sense of the flow and flavor of Jewish history? Do you know enough to begin to create Jewish memories?"

A woman who was responsible for cleaning out the house of her recently deceased mother once told me, "The sterling silver meant nothing to me. The minks in the closet meant nothing to me. When I saw the *haggadot* that we used at our seders, I broke down crying."

She had found the sanctuary of Jewish memory.

A Sanctuary Of Jewish Learning

Saturday morning after Saturday morning, week after week, in synagogues all over the continent, thirteen-year-olds make beautiful speeches about Jewish responsibility, the value of Jewish learning, and the importance of the synagogue. In almost half the cases, those pious incantations are soon forgotten. Post- bar and bat mitzvah Jewish education is an American Jewish scandal.

The home, which has surrendered its role to the media and the popular culture, must once again be a moral agent. It is not that we are raising our children to be immoral. We are not raising them to consider the essential, indispensable questions that go beyond the self and, even, beyond the family.

Continuing Jewish education is linked to personal integrity. Your children can intuit whether or not you take the covenantal nature of bar and bat mitzvah seriously. What they learn from you will stay with them the rest of their lives. Ancient rabbis believed that children develop a conscience no later than the thirteenth year. "Bar mitzvah" or "bat mitzvah" means, then, one who is "old enough to have a conscience." We must therefore be careful of the messages we send. Every child who reads from a Torah scroll at a bar or bat mitzvah— and then never returns to Jewish education—has learned a lesson in manipulating truth.

Remaining involved with Jewish education also teaches teenagers the value of staying with a task until it is finished. As a professor at an elite women's college said, "For parents to teach students that certain things can be done inadequately or incompletely [e.g., Jewish education and activities] ultimately does damage to the student. They become *comfortable* with mediocrity. There has to be an internalized message: whatever you do, *do well."*

Dropping out of Jewish education after bar and bat mitzvah mocks all that bar and bat mitzvah stands for—Jewish learning and its power to shape and influence our lives.

No Jewish community that could assimilate while living in freedom survived if it was Jewishly illiterate and uninformed. Such communities, such people are like cut flowers that wither and die. They need their tradition for spiritual sustenance and moral nourishment.

One of the best arguments for high quality Jewish education that I have ever read comes from the pen of Mark Jacobson. In the "Ethics" column of *Esquire* magazine, he struggled with whether to give his children a Jewish education:

> The notion of someone being "empty-headed" doesn't exist anymore. These days, you watch TV, go to the movies, your head gets filled up. It gets filled up with junk, but junk takes up room like anything else, and it tends to have a nasty half-life. . . .

> Like any well-intentioned dad, I seek to protect my children from what I consider detrimental. That's why, with increasing urgency, I'm turning to religion. If a mythic value system is going to be involuntarily absorbed by a kid of mine, I'd rather it be a 2,500-year-old mythos, the product of the constant working and reworking of the most creative minds of a society, than a tinny narrative worked up during a twenty-minute meeting in a sleek-lined NBC story conference room.

There is no such thing as a person without a story. There is no such thing as a person without a tribe. We are now only obliged to ask: Which story do we want our children to know? Which story do we want them to tell to their children? To which tribe do we want them to belong?

Broken idols are the building blocks of the sanctuary of Jewish learning. The idol of *competitiveness* leads us to evaluate our lives based on what we own. The idol of *entitlement* says that the world owes me everything. The idol of *elitism* says, "I deserve what I got, and those that don't got don't deserve it, anyway."

Consider the values that are implicit in what the Jewish people have taught over the centuries.

Too many now give minimally or begrudgingly to charity, or give vastly inflated contributions as overblown ego trips. Yet, the Jewish tradition teaches the concept of *tzedakah* as justice. It is what we must do as part of our covenant with God.

Our world says, "Me first." Yet, Jewish tradition teaches *gemilut chasadim* (acts of loving kindness).

Ours is a disposable fast food world of Whoppers, Coke, wrappers, and styrofoam. Yet, Jewish tradition teaches the beauty of *challah* and wine on Shabbat, served on the best china on a dining room table covered with the whitest of white tablecloths to bring honor to Shabbat. Suddenly the table is no longer *just* a table. It is a *mikdash me-at,* a sanctuary in miniature, a memory of the ancient Temple in Jerusalem. And it is in our home. And it transforms us.

Our world has reduced communication to gossip and innuendo. Yet, Jewish tradition teaches that the most beautiful words we can utter are words of *tefilah,* of prayer, and of the sacred learning of Torah.

Our world cultivates a certain amnesia about the past. Yet, Jewish tradition teaches that memory is the path to holiness.

Our world has enthroned the scant information that comes from sound bytes. Yet, Judaism teaches ancient wisdom from a scroll that one person wrote painstakingly by hand.

There is a certain weightiness and glory and power to this tradition. Even when parents cannot fully articulate it, they know it to be true. On a Shabbat morning many years ago, I helped a young man who was becoming bar mitzvah. He entered into Jewish maturity before the eyes of a small but loving congregation. As his father blessed him, he said these most poignant of words: "May I be the last ignorant Jew in this family."

The Sanctuary Of The Spirit

If God is truly on the guest list at our bar or bat mitzvah ceremony, that divine presence will resound through the years. If God is not on the guest list, then we and our young people will notice. Maybe not right away, but God's absence will be noticed.

On the Friday after a recent Thanksgiving, a young man who was a sophomore in college made an appointment to see me in my office. We had never met before. He had become bar mitzvah at my synagogue years before I had arrived. "Bar mitzvah, for me and my friends," he said, ". . . was a big party and expensive gifts and a lot of questions about 'How much did you make?' I looked back on it and said to myself, 'Where was the religious grandeur and the power?' I rebelled. At college, I've gotten involved with Native Americans. Their spirituality and religious ecstasy is what I've always wanted to find in Judaism.

"I went on the Sacred Run to support the rights of Native Americans. We ran across Canada and across Europe. Somehow we wound up at Auschwitz. My Native American friends said to me, 'This is your tribe's place of overwhelming darkness. Will you lead us in a ceremony at this place?'

"I didn't know what to say. I called my mother collect—from Auschwitz!—and asked her to find the prayerbook that I got when I became bar mitzvah. It was somewhere in my room. Then I asked her to read me the transliteration of the Kaddish prayer, so that I could write it down and say it at Auschwitz.

"Rabbi," he said, "I want to come back to my people. I really want to find that spirit again. My Native American friends sent me back to my tribe."

The prophet Isaiah knew what he was doing when he named one of his children *Shear Yashuv* ("a remnant will return"). A remnant will. A remnant has.

Bar mitzvah and bat mitzvah can be the gateway for our young people into their tribe, into their moral wisdom, into their sense of the Eternal.

Our young are ready to emerge from bar or bat mitzvah as different people, ready to shatter idols, ready to build sanctuaries.

Help them.

Sit down with your teenager and come up with a list of Jewish values that you would like to become part of their moral vocabularies. What are some concrete actions that will bring your teenager to that goal? Write them down here.

A P P E N D I C E S

1
What Non-Jews Should Know About The Bar And Bat Mitzvah Service

2
A List Of Places For Your Tzedakah

APPENDIX 1
What Non-Jews Should Know About The Bar And Bat Mitzvah Service

This appendix restates some of the material found in earlier chapters. It is an explanation of the bar and bat mitzvah that you can send to non-Jewish guests with their invitations.

Jews and Christians look at many things differently. We have a different theology, a different liturgy, a different holiday cycle, and a different life cycle.

But Jews and Christians share certain things, and that sharing is no less profound than the differences. As philosopher Martin Buber once said, "Jews and Christians share a Book and a hope"—a Messianic hope. Jews and Christians "share" the first five books of the Bible. We both believe in a God that can be approached through prayer and worship. We believe in a God who loves and who is revealed through Scripture and holy interventions in history.

Jews and Christians also share a belief in the power of ritual. Rituals make a group distinctive and transmit identity from generation to generation. They dramatize a religious group's beliefs about the world and about how God interacts with it.

Bar and bat mitzvah means that a thirteen-year-old Jewish child is old enough to perform *mitzvot* (the commandments of Jewish life). It is one of the most venerable and most potent of Jewish symbols and rituals. When a Jewish child becomes bar or bat mitzvah, he or she publicly reads a section from the Torah, the Five Books of Moses. Each week, every congregation in the Jewish world reads the identical passage. In this way, the youth is linked to the entire Jewish people, regardless of where the thirteen-year-old happens to live. The youth also reads a *haftarah,* which is a selection from the weekly section of the prophetic writings—from Isaiah, Amos, Hosea, etc., or from historical books like Joshua, Judges, Samuel, or Kings.

There is More to the Service than Meets The Ear

The bar and bat mitzvah ceremony occurs during the Sabbath worship service. The first part of the service ends with the congregation singing *Mi Chamocha* ("Who is like You among the gods?"). It echoes the song that Moses and the Israelites sang at the shores of the Red Sea when the Israelites had been saved from the Egyptians. The second part of the service ends with a prayer for peace for the Jewish people and for the whole world. During the third section of the service, the Torah is read. The *haftarah,* by tradition, must end on a note of *nechemta* (comfort). This portion of the service ends with the implicit hope that all humanity will embrace God's words.

The entire service concludes with two prayers: *Aleinu,* a triumphant plea that the world will *ultimately* recognize that there is only one God, and *Kaddish,* a plaintive mourners' prayer which proclaims that God's rule, the fulfillment of God's hopes for the world, will come someday. Kaddish's form and function are closely related to the Lord's Prayer.

The ultimate message of the service is *the triumph of hope:* hope for freedom, hope for peace, hope that all our words will end on joyful notes, hope for universal redemption.

There Is More To The Torah Scroll Than Meets The Eye

The Torah symbolizes the moment when God met the Jewish people at Sinai and made a covenant with them. It reminds us of God's revelation and of God's intervention in human history.

The Torah also symbolizes all that the Jewish people hold sacred: stories, laws, histories, poetry. When a Jewish child reads from the Torah, he or she is enveloped in its heritage, in its power, in the majesty of Sinai. He or she says to the community: "I am now thirteen years old. I am now ready to fulfill the covenant with God by being responsible for performing *mitzvot,* the obligations of Jewish life."

All Ritual Moments Of Becoming Are More Or Less Alike

All religions—all cultures—have their moments of *becoming.* It is a moment when an individual goes from childhood to maturity, a moment of sacred initiation.

Bar and bat mitzvah have certain parallels in Christianity. In the Baptist tradition, *baptism* itself is that moment of becoming. Baptism occurs during young adulthood rather than infancy because only then, Baptists believe, can one freely assent to Christianity.

In most Christian denominations, the closest parallel to bar and bat mitzvah is *confirmation*. Confirmation acknowledges a mature entry into the rites and the embrace of the church. It ratifies the baptismal vows that had been made for the child in infancy, just as bar and bat mitzvah acknowledge the pledge the parents made when their child was an infant that their child would study Torah.

Bar and bat mitzvah is a symbolic way to usher a child into the adult Jewish community, a way for the entire community to say to that no-longer-child, "All we cherish, all we hope to be, the sum total of our visions, we place them in your hands. May God make you ready. May God make you strong."

APPENDIX 2
A List of Places For Your Tzedakah

The following is a list of organizations that do worthwhile mitzvot. *It can be used in a number of ways. Your child may choose to give part of his or her bat or bat mitzvah gift money to a particular organization whose work is meaningful to your family. You may choose to put certain organizations on a list that will accompany the bar or bat mitzvah invitations, suggesting that your guests donate to the groups of their choice in honor of the bar or bat mitzvah. Or, your family may volunteer for the organization and enrich the bar and bat mitzvah experience by making it an experiment in living* mitzvot.

- *Soup kitchens for the homeless.* Soup kitchens feed the poor and the homeless. Sometimes, they feed entire families. Donate leftovers from your bar or bat mitzvah celebration. Consider how much smoked salmon and salad is thrown out on any Saturday afternoon after a bar and bat mitzvah party, and then consider how many hungry people walk around the streets of even the poshest suburbs. It doesn't have to be that way. To find your local food bank, consult the "Social and Human Services" section of your Yellow Pages.

Some notable food banks:

Mary Brennan Interfaith Nutrition Network (INN), 146-148 Front Street, Hempstead, NY 11550. (516) 486-8506.

Long Island Cares, Inc., P.O. Box 1073, West Brentwood, NY 11717. (516) 435-0454—food bank, (516) 435-1936—administrative office. Operates the Long Island Regional Food Bank which distributes huge quantities of donated food to soup kitchens and hunger organizations throughout Long Island.

Yad Ezra Kosher Food Pantry, 26641 Harding, Oak Park, MI 48237. (313) 548-3663.

Rachel's Table, 633 Salisbury Street, Worcester, MA 01609. (508) 799-7600. Picks up leftovers from *simchas* and distributes it to the needy.

Hebrew Union College, Brookdale Center, 1 West 4th Street, New York, NY 10012. (212) 674-5300. Attention: Dr. Lawrence Raphael, Dean of Administration. A one-night-a-week program to feed the homeless.

Passover Fund, B'nai B'rith Project Hope, c/o Len Elenowitz, 8801 Post Oak Road, Potomac, MD 20854. (301) 983-1345. Delivers Passover packages to Washington-area Jews.

- *Local Soviet Jewry committees.* These groups often include the most caring, dynamic, altruistic members of the Jewish community. Call your local Jewish federation or Jewish community center for information on locating your local Soviet Jewry committee, or contact the National Conference on Soviet Jewry—1522 K Street, N.W., Suite 1100, Washington, DC 20005. (202) 898-2500—for details on the nearest chapter to you.

- *Agencies that help the home-bound Jewish elderly.* Many aged live in utter isolation in bleak apartments with multiple locks on their doors. The conditions in which they live is a scandal, and their numbers are larger than most people think. Agencies organized to help these individuals include:

Dorot, 171 West 85th Street, New York, NY 10025. (212) 769-2850. Dorot means "generations"—generations of Jews together bringing light into lives that would have been otherwise darkened. Dorot operates a soup kitchen and distributes clothing to home-bound elderly Jews.

Hatzilu, 44 East 89th Street, Brooklyn, NY 11236. (718) 485-4142. Aids the Jewish poor and elderly of Brooklyn, Queens, and Long Island.

The Ark, 6450 N. California Avenue, Chicago, IL 60645. (312) 973-1000. Offers extensive services to poor Jews, including dental and medical care, employment counseling, a food pantry, and help in navigating the social service bureaucracy.

Sunday Jewish Food Program, Federation Homes, 156 Wintonbury Avenue, Bloomfield, CT 06002. (203) 243-2535. Offers a Sunday kosher meal program to many Jews in the greater Hartford area.

Other organizations that do worthy things:

ARMDI: American Red Magen David for Israel, 888 Seventh Avenue, Suite 403, New York, NY 10106. (212) 757-1627. The sole support arm in the United States for the Magen David, Israel's emergency medical and blood services organization.

American Jewish World Service, 15 West 26th Street, 9th floor, New York, NY 10010. (212) 683-1161. Has become the Jewish response to suffering caused by famine, epidemic, or natural disaster. The group has managed projects in Africa, South America, Mexico, and the United States.

American Rabbinic Network for Ethiopian Jewry, 859 South Oakland Avenue, Pasadena, CA 91106. (213) 681-4065. Thousands of Ethiopian Jews have emigrated to Israel, but many still remain in Ethiopia. ARNEJ keeps them in our consciousness through education, fund-raising, and "twinning" opportunities for bar and bat mitzvah.

Bet Tzedek, 145 S. Fairfax Avenue, Suite #200, Los Angeles, CA 90036. (213) 939-0506. Provides free legal work for poor Jews and non-Jews. Has produced a video, narrated by actress Bea Arthur, which portrays six examples of their work.

The Eldridge Street Project, 12 Eldridge Street, New York, NY 10002. (212) 219-0888. Established to preserve and restore the Eldridge Street Synagogue, one of the most beautiful older synagogues of New York City. Also plans to establish a Jewish historic cultural district on the Lower East Side. Deserves *tzedakah* because it preserves a valuable piece of our past.

The Foundation to Sustain Righteous Christians, c/o Rabbi Harold Schulweis, Valley Beth Shalom, 15739 Ventura Blvd., Encino, CA 91436. (818) 788-6000. Many Christians who saved Jews from the Nazis now live in poverty in the United States, Europe, and Israel. Jews must remember them; our history is incomplete without them. The foundation sustains them financially and emotionally, thus bearing witness to eternal gratitude.

God's Love We Deliver, 895 Amsterdam Avenue, New York, NY 10025. (212) 865-4900. Prepares and delivers meals for people with AIDS.

Interns for Peace, 270 West 89th Street, New York, NY 10024. (212) 580-0540. This apolitical organization trains workers to help Arabs and Jews develop common interests, hoping these will erode the walls of bigotry.

North American Jewish Student's Appeal, 165 Pidgeon Hill Road, Huntington Station, NY 11746. (516) 385-8771. Provides supplemental funds to several Jewish student groups on campuses around the country: the Bayit project, which establishes Jewish residences on campus; the Progressive Zionist Caucus, which promotes pluralism in Israel; various Jewish student newspapers, seminars and projects.

Mazon, 2940 Westwood Boulevard, Suite 7, Los Angeles, CA 90064. (213) 470-7769. Asks Jews to send three percent of the cost of a *simcha* to MAZON so we can share our blessing with the needy. MAZON then makes allocations to hunger organizations around the country.

National Institute for Jewish Hospice, 8723 Alden Drive, Suite #652, Los Angeles, CA 90048. (213) 854-3036. The only national Jewish organization providing non-hospital alternatives for the terminally ill. Hospice is a place where people go to die with dignity and appropriate care.

The Jewish Braille Institute of America, 110 East 30th Street, New York, NY 10016. (212) 889-2525. Provides books, tapes, special materials for summer camps, college and career counselling, and free *benei mitzvah* training to blind and partially sighted Jewish adults. Improves the quality of Jewish life for the estimated 20,000 Jewish blind and 50,000 Jews who are severely visually impaired.

The New Israel Fund, 111 West 40th Street, Suite 2300, New York, NY 10018. (212) 302-0066. Funds the following programs in Israel: Jewish/Arab relations; pluralism; civil rights and civil liberties; women's rights, especially rape crisis centers; and community action.

United Jewish Appeal—Federation of Jewish Philanthropies, 130 East 59th Street, New York, NY 10022. (212) 980-1000. Most comprehensive Jewish charity in the world. Raises almost $750 million annually from American Jews to serve the world-wide needs of Jews. Jewish elderly on the Lower East side, Jewish farmers in the Galilee, Jews in Eastern Europe and Moslem nations all benefit. Giving to the UJA is absolutely essential for every serious Jew's *tzedakah* plans.

Israel Bonds. This and the UJA are the great international pillars of support for Israel. Israel's capital improvements and infrastructure are largely the result of the strong commitment to Israel Bonds by Jews all over the world. Not just *tzedakah*—it's an investment in Israel's future.

Simon Wiesenthal Center, 9760 West Pico Boulevard, Los Angeles, CA 90035. (213) 553-9036. Has taken a leading role in discovering Nazis in hiding as well as exposing modern hate groups. Insures that Americans will remember the Holocaust.

Trevor's Campaign for the Homeless, 3415 Westchester Pike, Suite #201, Newtown Square, PA 19073. (215) 642-6452. Trevor Ferrell, now an adult, began his "campaign" at the age of eleven. Includes a nightly food run, a shelter, housing for women and children, and day-care.

The National Yiddish Book Center, P.O. Box 969, Amherst, MA 01004. (413) 256-1241. Yiddish must survive, and more than in vulgar humor or small catch-phrases. By finding, saving, and treasuring Yiddish books, the Book Center redeems a small part of the Jewish past.

Lifeline for the Old—Yad LaKashish, 14 Shivtei Yisrael Street, Jerusalem, 287-829. Created so Jerusalem's elderly would create lovely handicrafts, *challah* covers, *talitot,* toys, metal *mezuzot,* ceramic items, clothing, book binding. Also employs young and old handicapped individuals. Contributions can be sent to American Friends of Lifeline for the Old in Israel, c/o Florence Schiffman, 1500 Palisades Avenue., Fort Lee, NJ 07024. (201) 947-2140.

• *Shelters for battered Jewish women.* Provide temporary shelter, counseling, and support services to Jewish women who are victims of domestic violence. Examples include:

Rebbetzin Chana Weinberg, 398 Mt. Wilson Lane, Baltimore, MD 21208. (301) 486-0322. Operates one of less than ten Jewish battered women's shelters in North America. Contributions should be made out to Chana Weinberg Tzedakah Fund.

Shalva, 1610 W. Highland, Chicago, IL 60660. (312) 583-HOPE. Founded by Orthodox women who worked in a *mikveh* (ritual bath) and noticed scars on the women they were tending.

Ziv Tzedakah Fund, 11818 Trail Ridge Drive, Potomac, MD 20854. This is the independent *tzedakah* fund of Danny Siegel: poet, writer, and *mitzvah* impresario. He searches for and finds righteous people doing holy work and raises money for them.

With thanks to Rabbi Marc Gellman and Danny Siegel, who suggested many of the tzedakot *on this list.*

GO AND LEARN:
Resources for Parents

The following list comprises what I believe to be the best and most accessible books on Judaism for the lay reader. Any of these would be an excellent way to continue your Jewish learning and can be used to help deepen the bar and bat mitzvah experience.

"What are the best books about Jews who have gone on spiritual searches?"

Cowan, Paul. *An Orphan in History: Retrieving a Jewish Legacy.* Garden City, NJ: Doubleday and Co., Inc., 1982. Paul Cowan, of blessed memory, was an activist and writer for New York's *Village Voice.* This book chronicles his return to his Jewish roots.

Goldman, Ari. *The Search for God at Harvard.* New York: Random House, 1991. Goldman, religion editor of *The New York Times,* takes a sabbatical to study at the Harvard Divinity School. There he learns that "if you know one religion, you don't know *any* religion!" This book describes his experiences.

Ochs, Vanessa L. *Words on Fire: One Woman's Journey into the Sacred.* New York: Harcourt Brace Jovanovich, 1990. One woman's experience of a return to Jewish texts and wisdom—in the *yeshivah* world of Jerusalem.

Roiphe, Anne. *Generation without Memory: A Jewish Journey in Christian America.* Boston: Beacon Press, 1981. An assimilated Jewish woman discovers what she has been missing Jewishly all those years. A chronicle of Jewish growth.

"I'd like to be able to tell my family some Jewish stories. Where can I learn some?"

Epstein, Lawrence J. *A Treasury of Jewish Anecdotes.* Northvale, NJ: Jason Aronson, 1989.

Frankel, Ellen. *The Classic Tales: Four Thousand Years of Jewish Lore.* Northvale, NJ: Jason Aronson, 1989.

Gellman, Marc. *Does God Have a Big Toe?* New York: Harper and Row, 1989.

Schwartz, Howard. *Elijah's Violin and Other Jewish Fairy Tales.* New York: Harper and Row, 1983.

"I'd like to think more about what it means to raise Jewish children."

Bell, Roselyn, ed. *The Hadassah Magazine Jewish Parenting Book.* New York: The Free Press, 1989. An anthology on various issues, including Jewish education and bar and bat mitzvah.

Donin, Hayim Halevy. *To Raise a Jewish Child: A Guide to Parents.* New York: Basic Books, 1980. The traditional Jewish point of view on the topic.

Kurshan, Neil. *Raising Your Child to Be a Mensch.* New York: Atheneum MacMillan Publishing Company, 1987. Written for a general audience, but grounded in Jewish values and texts.

"Bar and bat mitzvah has raised some important questions about intermarriage and conversion."

Cowan, Paul and Rachel. *Mixed Blessings: Marriage Between Jews and Christians.* New York: Doubleday, 1987. The classic book on the challenges of interfaith marriages. Rachel Cowan ultimately converted to Judaism and is now a Reform rabbi. I give this book to interfaith couples with whom I work. It has changed more than a few lives.

Kukoff, Lydia. *Choosing Judaism.* New York: Union of American Hebrew Congregation, 1981. The classic story of a woman who converted to Judaism and whose life inspired thousands of non-Jews looking for spiritual sustenance in Judaism.

Mayer, Egon. *Love and Tradition: Marriage between Jews and Christians.* New York: Plenum Publishing Corporation, 1985. The best in-depth reportage and analysis of intermarriage in American Jewish life, by one of the master sociologists of American Jewry.

Romanoff, Lena, with Lisa Holstein. *Your People, My People: Finding Acceptance and Fulfillment as a Jew by Choice.* Philadelphia: Jewish Publication Society, 1990. Challenges and pitfalls of converting to Judaism.

Schneider, Susan Weidman. *Intermarriage: The Challenge of Living with Differences between Jews and Christians.* New York: Free Press, 1989. Thoughtful discussion of major issues connected with intermarriage.

"I'd like to learn more about the Jewish worship service."

Donin, Hayim Halevy. *To Pray as a Jew: A Guide to the Prayerbook and the Synagogue Service.* New York: Basic Books, 1980. A detailed description of the traditional Jewish worship service.

Hoffman, Lawrence. *The Art of Public Prayer: Not for Clergy Only.* Washington, DC: Pastoral Press, 1989. One of the most important books about Jewish worship. Asks why do services "work," and how can the worship experience be saved?

"The bar or bat mitzvah experience has made me more curious about Bible and Torah."

Greeley, Andrew M. and Jacob Neusner. *The Bible and Us: A Priest and a Rabbi Read Scripture Together.* New York: Warner Books, 1990. Two prolific scholars examine the joint inheritance of the Hebrew Bible, with due attention also paid to the New Testament.

Hertz, J. H. *The Pentateuch and Haftorahs.* London: Soncino Press, 1972. The classic Torah commentary, found in the pews of many synagogues.

Plaut, W. Gunther, ed. *A Torah: A Modern Commentary.* New York: Union of American Hebrew Congregations, 1981. The first Torah commentary produced and published in North America. The articles on each Torah portion and the pages called "Gleanings," containing insights from the tradition, are extremely valuable.

Rosenberg, David, ed. *Congregation: Contemporary Writers Read the Jewish Bible.* New York: Harcourt Brace Jovanovitch, 1987. Modern Jewish writers read each book of the Hebrew Bible. Sometimes brilliant, sometimes outrageous, always interesting.

Visotsky, Burton L. *Reading the Book: Making the Bible a Timeless Text.* New York: Anchor Books, 1991. Lively inquiry into Biblical literature through the lens of rabbinic midrash.

"I'd like to learn more about the history of Jewish literature."

Holtz, Barry W. *Back to the Sources: Reading the Classic Jewish Texts.* New York: Summit Books, 1984. Essays on the different genres of classic Jewish literature: Bible, Talmud, Midrash, Hasidism, philosophy, etc.

____. *Finding Our Way: Jewish Texts and the Lives We Lead Today.* New York: Schocken, 1990. Concerned with the social and religious implications of classic texts.

Siegel, Danny. *Where Heaven and Earth Touch.* Northvale, NJ: Jason Aronson, 1989. The best topical collection of Jewish texts assembled in recent years.

"I need some clear reference books on Jewish concepts and terminology."

Bulka, Reuven P. *What You Thought You Knew About Judaism: 341 Common Misconceptions About Jewish Life.* Northvale, NJ: Jason Aronson, 1989. A playful refutation of common misconceptions about Judaism.

Klagsbrun, Francine. *Voices of Wisdom: Jewish Ideals and Ethics for Everyday Living.* New York: Pantheon Books, 1980. An anthology of Jewish wisdom.

Telushkin, Joseph. *Jewish Literacy: The Most Important Things to Know about the Jewish Religion, Its People, and Its History.* New York: William Morrow and Co., 1991. The best one-volume introduction to Judaism in recent years. Written with joy, humor, and authenticity. Truly "entry level" and highly recommended.

"I need some good basic books on observing Jewish holidays and life cycle events."

Greenberg, Irving. *The Jewish Way: Living the Holidays.* New York: Summit, 1988. One of the great modern Orthodox scholars and leaders of our time explains the inner dynamics of the holiday cycle. Masterful.

Klein, Isaac. *A Guide to Jewish Religious Practice.* New York: KTAV, 1979. Considered by some to be the "state of the art" guide to Jewish practice for Conservative Jews, yet contains riches for Jews in all movements.

Knobel, Peter. *Gates of the Seasons: A Guide to the Jewish Year.* New York: Central Conference of American Rabbis, 1983. An outline of the *mitzvot* of the holiday cycle, written from a Reform perspective.

Maslin, Simeon. *Gates of Mitzvah: A Guide to the Jewish Life Cycle.* New York: Central Conference of American Rabbis, 1979. An outline of the *mitzvot* of the life cycle, written from a Reform perspective.

Shapiro, Mark Dov. *Gates of Shabbat: A Guide for Observing Shabbat.* New York: Central Conference of American Rabbis, 1991. An entry point for all serious non-Orthodox Jews.

Strassfeld, Michael. *The Jewish Holidays: A Guide and Commentary.* New York: Harper and Row, 1985. Continues in the style of the *Catalog.*

Strassfeld, Sharon and Michael; Siegel, Richard. *The Jewish Catalog.* 3 volumes. Philadelphia: Jewish Publication Society. Classic works on modern Jewish observance.

Syme, Daniel B. *The Jewish Home.* New York: Union of American Hebrew Congregations, 1988. Holiday and life cycle observance is presented in a question-and-answer format.

"I'd like to learn more about modern Jewish theology."

Eugene B. Borowitz. *Choices in Modern Jewish Thought: A Partisan Guide.* New York: Behrman House, 1983. Elucidates Buber, Rosenzweig, Heschel, Kaplan, etc.

_____ . *Liberal Judaism.* New York: Union of American Hebrew Congregations, 1984. Classic work on Reform Judaism's beliefs.

_____ . *Renewing the Covenant: A Theology for the Postmodern Jew.* Philadelphia: Jewish Publication Society, 1991. Perhaps the best book ever written on contemporary Jewish theology.

Cohen, Arthur A. and Paul Mendes-Flohr, eds. *Contemporary Jewish Religious Thought.* New York: Charles Scribner's Sons, 1987. A sophisticated one-volume encyclopedia of Jewish theological issues. Many essays are gems of Jewish thought.

Feld, Edward. *The Spirit of Renewal: Crisis and Response in Jewish Life.* Woodstock, VT: Jewish Lights Publishing, 1991. Examines key transitional moments in ancient and modern Jewish history and seeks to understand their theological implications.

Gillman, Neil. *Sacred Fragments: Recovering Theology for the Modern Jew.* Philadelphia: Jewish Publication Society, 1990. Great, accessible outlines of Jewish positions on revelation, authority, eschatology, etc.

Green, Arthur. *Seek My Face, Speak My Name: A Contemporary Jewish Theology.* Northvale, NJ: Jason Aronson, 1992. Green, the president of the Reconstructionist Rabbinical College, creates a modern theology that listens to the insights of Jewish mysticism and Chasidism, and yet speaks to the spiritual needs of the contemporary moment.

Kushner, Harold. *Who Needs God.* New York: Summit Books, 1989. Good for those with deep questions about God.

Schulweis, Harold. *In God's Mirror: Reflections and Essays.* Hoboken, NJ: KTAV, 1990. Essays on Jewish life and thought. Poetic and pointed.

Wolpe, David J. *The Healer of Shattered Hearts: A Jewish View of God.* New York: Henry Holt and Company, 1990. A young scholar points to where God might be found.

"I'm curious about the Jewish mystical search and spirituality. What are some good books to read?"

Kushner, Lawrence. *The Book of Letters.* Woodstock, VT: Jewish Lights Publishing, 1990.

_____. *The Book of Miracles: Jewish Spirituality for Children to Read to Their Parents and Parents to Read to Their Children.* New York: Union of American Hebrew Congregations Press, 1987.

_____. *God Was In This Place and I, i Did Not Know: Finding Self, Spirituality, and Ultimate Meaning.* Woodstock, VT: Jewish Lights Publishing, 1991.

_____. *Honey From The Rock.* Woodstock, VT: Jewish Lights Publishing, 1990.

_____. *The River of Light: Spirituality, Judaism, Consciousness.* Woodstock, VT: Jewish Lights Publishing, 1990.

Kushner's books are the best introduction to Jewish spirituality for the lay reader.

"What are some good books that will give me and my family some more ideas about tzedakah and mitzvah projects?"

Siegel, Danny. *Gym Shoes and Irises: Personalized Tzedakah* (Books 1 and 2). Spring Valley, NY: The Town House Press, 1982, 1987.

_____. *Munbaz II and Other Mitzvah Heroes.* Spring Valley, NY: The Town House Press, 1988.

_____. *Mitzvahs.* Pittsboro, NC: The Townhouse Press, 1990.

Siegel's books contain more ideas for *tzedakah* than one could possibly do in a lifetime. Siegel, a poet, turns *mitzvah*-doing into a poetry of the Jewish soul.

Glossary

aliyah (plural, *aliyot*): literally, "going up." The ascent to the *bimah* to say the blessings over the Torah scroll.

amidah: literally, the "standing" prayer. The nineteen prayers that constitute the main body of Jewish liturgy; also known as *tefilah* and the *shemoneh esrei*.

Baruch shepetarani me-onsho shel zeh: Blessing traditionally uttered by the father at the occasion of his son becoming bar mitzvah: "Blessed is The One Who has now freed me from responsibility for this one."

bikur cholim: visiting the sick.

bimah: the raised platform in most synagogues where the service is conducted.

chesed: loving kindness.

chumash (from *chameish,* "five'): the Pentateuch (Five Books of Moses), or a book containing the Pentateuch.

derashah: a brief exposition of the Torah portion for the week. Sometimes referred to as the *devar Torah,* "a word of Torah."

haftarah: literally, "completion." The reading of the section from the Prophets for a particular Shabbat.

halachah: literally, "the going." Traditional Jewish law.

havdalah: literally, "separation," "distinction." The ceremony that ends Shabbat.

kavvanah: sacred intention, the goal of Jewish prayer and worship.

ketuvim: the third section of the Hebrew Bible *(Tanach).* Includes Psalms, Proverbs, Job, Song of Songs, Ruth, Lamentations, Ecclesiastes, Esther.

midrash: literally, "the searching out." A post-biblical, rabbinic interpretation of a Biblical verse.

mikra: the Hebrew Bible.

mincha: the afternoon Jewish worship service.

Mishnah: the classic post-biblical code of Jewish law, compiled in Israel circa 200 C.E. by Rabbi Judah Ha-nasi (Judah the Prince).

mitzvah (plural, *mitzvot*): an obligation of Jewish life.

musaf: the "additional" prayer in traditional liturgy. Recalls the ancient sacrificial rites of the Temple (the *musaf* or additional sacrifices) and repeats some themes covered earlier in the liturgy.

neviim: the second section of the Hebrew Bible *(Tanach)*. Consists of the prophetic and historical writings.

nichum aveilim: the *mitzvah* of comforting mourners.

parasha: the Torah portion of the week. Also sometimes referred to as the *sedra*.

parochet: the curtain that hung before the Holy of Holies in the ancient Temple in Jerusalem. Now refers to the curtain that hangs before the *aron hakodesh* (the Ark) in the synagogue.

pidyon shevuim: the *mitzvah* of redeeming captives.

Pirke Avot: literally, "the chapters of the fathers." The ethical maxims of the Mishnah, as quoted in the names of the early Rabbis.

Shulchan Aruch: literally, "the set table." The sixteenth-century code of Jewish law compiled by Joseph Caro.

Talmud: literally, "learning." Commentaries and discussions of the Mishnah, compiled circa 450 C.E.-500 C.E. One Talmud was compiled in Palestine (the Palestinian or Jerusalem Talmud, known as the *Yerushalmi*); the more authoritative one was compiled in Babylonia (the Babylonian Talmud, known as the *Bavli*).

Tanach: acronym for *Torah, Neviim* (the Prophets) and *Ketuvim* (the later Writings) that comprise the Hebrew Bible.

tefilah: the major section of Jewish liturgy. The generic term for Jewish worship.

Torah: literally, "teaching" or "direction." Narrowly, the first part of the Hebrew Bible that is read from the scroll; broadly, all Jewish sacred literature and by implication, all of Judaism.

tzedakah: the *mitzvah* of sacred giving.

Bibliography

Braunstein, Susan L. and Jenna Weissman Joselit. *Getting Comfortable in America: The American Jewish Home, 1880-1950.* New York: The Jewish Museum, 1990.

Capps, Donald. *Life Cycle Theory and Pastoral Care.* Philadelphia: Fortress Press, 1983.

Cohen, Alfred S. "Celebration of the Bat Mitzvah." *Journal of Halacha and Contemporary Society* 12 (Fall 1986/Sukkot 5747): 5-16.

Cohen, Arthur A. and Paul Mendes-Flohr, eds. *Contemporary Jewish Religious Thought.* New York: Charles Scribner's Sons, 1987.

Coles, Robert. *The Spiritual Life of Children.* Boston: Houghton Mifflin, 1990.

Douglas, Mary. *Natural Symbols: Explorations in Cosmology.* New York: Pantheon, 1982.

Eliade, Mircea. *Cosmos and History: The Myth of the Eternal Return.* New York: Harper and Row, 1954.

———. *Rites and Symbols of Initiation: The Mysteries of Birth and Rebirth.* New York: Harper Torchbooks, 1965.

Epstein, Isadore, trans. *The Babylonian Talmud.* London: Soncino Press, 1958.

Erikson, Erik H. *Childhood and Society.* New York: W. W. Norton, 1950.

Fein, Leonard. *Where Are We? The Inner Life of American Jews.* New York: Harper and Row, 1988.

Feuer, Leon I. "Second Thoughts About Bar-Bat Mitzvah," *Journal of Reform Judaism* 27, no. 1 (Winter 1980): 1-9.

Freedman, H., trans. *The Midrash Rabbah.* London: Soncino Press, 1977.

Freehof, Solomon B. *Recent Reform Responsa.* New York: KTAV, 1963.

Friedman, Edwin. *Generation to Generation: Family Process in Church and Synagogue.* New York: Guilford Press, 1985.

Glatzer, Nahum N., ed. *On Jewish Learning.* New York: Schocken Books, 1955.

Goldstein, Albert S. "Let's Bar Bar Mitzvah," *Central Conference of American Rabbis Journal* 3 (October 1953): 19-25.

Hall, Edward T. *Beyond Culture.* Garden City, NY: Anchor Books, 1976.

Heinemann, Joseph. *Literature of the Synagogue.* New York: Behrman House, 1975.

Hertzberg, Arthur. *The Jews in America.* New York: Simon and Schuster, 1989.

Heschel, Abraham Joshua. *Quest for God: Studies in Prayer and Symbolism.* New York: Crossroad, 1954.

Himmelfarb, Milton, ed. *The Condition of Jewish Belief: A Symposium Compiled by the Editors of Commentary Magazine.* Northvale, NJ: Jason Aronson, 1989.

Hoffman, Lawrence. *The Art of Public Prayer.* Washington, DC: Pastoral Press, 1989.

Jacob, Walter. "Initiation into Judaism." *Religious Education* 74, no. 6 (November-December 1979): 598-63.

————. ed. *American Reform Responsa: Collected Responsa of the Central Conference of American Rabbis, 1889-1983.* New York: Central Conference of American Rabbis, 1983.

Levinson, Daniel J. *The Seasons of a Man's Life.* New York: Ballantine Books, 1978.

Maimonides. *Mishneh Torah.* Warsaw-Vilna Edition, n.d.

Maslow, Abraham H. *Religions, Values, and Peak-Experiences.* London: Penguin Books, 1970.

Meyer, Michael. *Response to Modernity: A History of the Reform Movement in Judaism.* New York: Oxford University Press, 1988.

Midrash Rabbah. (Vilna edition). Jerusalem: 1975.

Neusner, Jacob. *The Enchantments of Judaism.* New York: Basic Books, 1987.

Orlean, Susan, *Saturday Night.* New York: Alfred A. Knopf, 1990.

Plaut, W. Gunther. *Tadrich L'Shabbat: A Shabbat Manual.* New York: Central Conference of American Rabbis, 1972.

Pogrebin, Letty Cottin. *Deborah, Golda, and Me: Being Female and Jewish in America.* New York: Crown Publishers, Inc., 1991.

Raphael, Marc Lee. *Profiles in American Judaism: The Reform, Conservative, Orthodox, and Reconstructionist Traditions in Historical Perspective.* San Francisco: Harper and Row, 1984.

Raphael, Ray. *The Men from the Boys: Rites of Passage in Male America.* Lincoln: University of Nebraska Press, 1990.

Roiphe, Anne. *Lovingkindness.* New York: Summit Books, 1987.

Roth, Cecil. *A History of the Marranos.* New York: Schocken Books, 1974.

Saperstein, Marc. *Jewish Preaching, 1200-1800: An Anthology.* New Haven, CT: Yale University Press, 1989.

Schauss, Hyman. *The Lifetime of the Jew.* New York: Union of American Hebrew Congregations, 1950.

Schulweis, Harold. *In God's Mirror: Reflections and Essays.* Hoboken, NJ: KTAV, 1990.

Sherwin, Byron L. *In Partnership with God: Contemporary Jewish Law and Ethics.* Syracuse: Syracuse University Press, 1990.

Silver, Daniel Jeremy. *The Story of Scripture: From Oral Tradition to the Written Word.* New York: Basic Books, 1990.

Slonimsky, Henry. *Essays.* Cincinnati: Hebrew Union College Press, 1967.

Snyder, Herman E. "Is Bar-Bat Mitzvah Destroying Attendance at Synagogue Services?" *Journal of Reform Judaism* 27, no. 1 (Winter 1980): 11-14.

Sofrim. Ed. Michael Higger, New York: Ginsburg, 1937.

Woocher, Jonathan S. *Sacred Survival: The Civil Religion of American Jews.* Bloomington: Indiana University Press, 1986.

Zborowski, Mark and Elizabeth Herzog. *Life Is with People.* New York: International Universities Press, 1952.

About JEWISH LIGHTS Publishing

People of all faiths and backgrounds yearn for books that attract, engage, educate and spiritually inspire.

Our principal goal is to stimulate thought and help all people learn about who the Jewish People are, where they come from, and what the future can be made to hold. While people of our diverse Jewish heritage are the primary audience, our books speak to the Christian world as well and will broaden their understanding of Judaism and the roots of their own faith.

We bring to you authors who are at the forefront of spiritual thought and experience. While each has something different to say, they all say it in a voice that you can hear.

Our books are designed to welcome you and then to engage, stimulate and inspire. We judge our success not only by whether or not our books are beautiful and commercially successful, but by whether or not they make a difference in your life.

We at Jewish Lights take great care to produce beautiful books that present meaningful spiritual content in a form that reflects the art of making high quality books. Therefore, we want to acknowledge those who contributed to the production of this book.

Art Direction and Production
Rachel Kahn

Art
Robert Lipnick, Davenport, Iowa

Calligraphy
Pamela Wasserman, Woodstock, Vermont

Text Format
Nancy Malerba, Weathersfield, Vermont

Type
Set in Bembo and Antique Olive
Barbara Homeyer Type, Inc., Lebanon, New Hampshire

Hebrew
Joel Hoffman, Excelsior Computer Services, Silver Spring, Maryland

Cover Printing
New England Book Components, Hingham, Massachusetts

Printing and Binding
Book Press, Inc., Brattleboro, Vermont

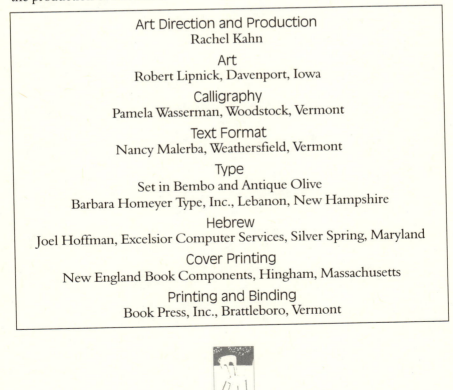

About The Art

Robert Lipnick is an American artist living in Davenport, Iowa. His work, considered Midwest Judaica, focuses on the themes of justice, genesis, the home, family, and nature. He has been commissioned by many families to create special artworks in commemoration of meaningful life cycle events. His ceramics and paintings are found in the collections of major museums and institutions throughout the world.

The images Lipnick uses on this book's cover are familiar to everyday Jewish life: family, Torah, prayer, Israel, love, and peace. The kiddush cup/tablets/mountains and the empty chair found in the cover art have been chosen as ornamentation for the text of the book. Together, they symbolize an invitation to all to celebrate while finding spiritual meaning in bar and bat mitzvah.

About The Hebrew Text

The text of the Hebrew prayers in *Putting God On The Guest List* were created by Joel Hoffman, Excelsior Computer Services, Silver Spring, Maryland, using "Servicemaker," a program he designed for IBM computers and compatibles. This program provides the user with all of the necessary step-by-step instructions to create a Jewish religious service. It includes the complete Hebrew and English texts for the major prayers, all necessary fonts, outlines, and detailed notes for each type of service.

Makes An Inspiring and Meaningful Bar or Bat Mitzvah Gift

THE BOOK OF LETTERS
A Mystical Hebrew Alphabet

by *Lawrence Kushner*

In calligraphy by the author. Folktales about and exploration of the mystical meanings of the Hebrew Alphabet. Open the old prayerbook-like pages of *The Book of Letters* and you will enter a special world of sacred tradition and religious feeling. More than just symbols, all twenty-two letters of the Hebrew alphabet overflow with meanings and personalities of their own.

Rabbi Kushner draws from ancient Judaic sources, weaving Talmudic commentary, Hasidic folktales, and Kabbalistic mysteries around the letters. Each letter is illuminated and, together with the comments, is presented in the author's original calligraphy, recalling the look and feel of ancient medieval manuscripts.

> "A book which is in love with Jewish letters. It gives us a feeling which the Kabbalists always knew—that the letters of the alphabet are not just letters but symbols of our history, of our philosophy, and of the life of the Jewish people. In this respect this book is unique." —Isaac Bashevis Singer (‎יל)

Popular Hardcover Edition

6"x 9", 80 pp. Hardcover, two colors, inspiring new Foreword.
ISBN 1-879045-00-1 **$24.95**

Deluxe Presentation Edition

- *Gold embossed slipcase.*
- *9"x 12" Deluxe Cloth Hardcover.*
- *Four-color printing illuminates 60 pages.*
- *Printed on a specially selected, premium laid-finish paper.*

9"x 12", 80 pp. ISBN 1-879045-01-X   **$79.95**

Collector's Limited Edition

A triumph of American craftsmanship, deserving of a place in the collections of those who are discerning enough to purchase or to give unusually fine artwork and books.

- *Limited to 500 signed and numbered copies.*
- *Exquisite gold foil embossing illuminates 60 pages.*
- *Designed and created by Rabbi Kushner and all in his own calligraphy.*
- *Accompanying each book is a magnificent frameable 11"x 14" limited edition silkscreened print, also signed and numbered.*

9"x 12", 80 pp. ISBN 1-879045-04-4 **$349.**

*To learn more about the Collector's Limited Edition
and to see a sample page at no obligation, call us.*

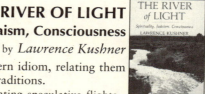

...oks from Jewish Lights

...H STEPS TO RECOVERY
...g From Alcoholism & Other Addictions

... Olitzky & Stuart A. Copans, MD
...MD • Introduction by *Rabbi Sheldon Zimmerman*
...tions by *Maty Grünberg*
...eps of addiction recovery programs offering consolation,
...y.
...ardcover, ISBN 1-879045-08-7 **$19.95**
...ity Paperback, ISBN 1-879045-09-5 **$12.95**

...NEWED EACH DAY
...Recovery Meditations Based on the Bible
...lume I: Genesis & Exodus

...bbi Kerry M. Olitzky & Aaron Z.
...i Michael Signer • Afterword by JACS Foundation

...: Leviticus, Numbers & Deuteronomy

...Rabbi Kerry M. Olitzky & Aaron Z.
...M. Strassfeld • Afterword by *Rabbi Harold M. Schulweis*

...guide format, a recovering person and a spiritual leader who
...d people reflect on the traditional weekly Torah reading.
..., 224 pp. Quality Paperback, ISBN 1-879045-12-5 **$12.95**
...", 320 pp. Quality Paperback, ISBN 1-879045-13-3 **$14.95**
...ipcased Set, Quality Paperback, ISBN 1-879045-21-4 **$27.90**

THE SPIRIT OF RENEWAL
Crisis & Response in Jewish Life

by *Edward Feld*

...landscape of Jewish religious thought after the Holocaust." In order
...on of faith after the Holocaust, Rabbi Feld places it within the con-
...great tragedy throughout Jewish history.
..."x 9", 208 pp. Hardcover, ISBN 1-879045-06-0 **$22.95**

GOD'S PAINTBRUSH

by *Sandy Eisenberg Sasso*
Full color illustrations by *Annette C. Compton*

..., involvement and the imagination, *God's Paintbrush* invites children of
...ackgrounds to encounter God. For all who wish to cultivate the religious
...encourage children to think and wonder about God. Non-sectarian.
...1"x 8½", 32 pp. Hardcover, Illus. , ISBN 1-879045-22-2 **$15.95**

SEEKING THE PATH TO LIFE
...ogical Meditations On The Nature Of God, Love, Life & Death

by *Rabbi Ira F. Stone*
Ornamentation by *Annie Stone*

...yet accessible series of personal meditations and theological discussions.
...he most basic human struggles: life and death, love and anger, peace and war,
cove... and exile.
6"x 9", 144 pp. Hardcover, ISBN 1-879045-17-6 **$19.95**

TORMENTED MASTER
The Life and Spiritual Quest of Rabbi Nahman of Bratslav

by *Arthur Green*

Explores the personality and religious quest of Nahman of Bratslav (1772–1810), one
of Hasidism's major figures. It unlocks the great themes of spiritual searching that
make him a figure of universal religious importance.
6"x 9", 408 pp. Quality Paperback, ISBN 1-879045-11-7 **$17.95**

Tree of Life Book Club

~Order Information~

Please send me the following book(s):

# Copies		$ Amount

The Book Of Letters
_____ Popular Hardcover Edition, $24.95 _____
_____ Deluxe Presentation Edition w/slipcase, $79.95, plus $5.95 s/h _____
_____ Collector's Limited Edition, $349.00, plus $12.50 s/h _____
_____ **God Was In This Place And I, i Did Not Know,** (hc) $21.95 _____
_____ **God's Paintbrush,** (hc) $15.95 _____
_____ **Honey From The Rock,** (pb) $14.95 _____
_____ **The Jerusalem Gates Portfolio,** $49.95 _____
_____ **Putting God On The Guest List,** (hc) $21.95 _____
_____ **Putting God On The Guest List,** (pb) $14.95 _____
_____ **Renewed Each Day,** Vol I, (pb) $12.95 _____
_____ **Renewed Each Day,** Vol II, (pb) $14.95 _____
_____ **Renewed Each Day,** 2-Volume Set, (pb) $27.90 _____
_____ **The River Of Light,** (pb) $14.95 _____
_____ **Seeking The Path To Life,** (hc) $19.95 _____
_____ **So That Your Values Live On,** (hc) $19.95 _____
_____ **Spirit Of Renewal,** (hc) $22.95 _____
_____ **Tormented Master,** (pb) $17.95 _____
_____ **Twelve Jewish Steps To Recovery,** (hc) $19.95 _____
_____ **Twelve Jewish Steps To Recovery,** (pb) $12.95 _____

For s/h, add $2.95 for the first book, $1 each additional book. _____

~~~ • ~~~ **Total** _____

Check enclosed for $_____ _payable to:_ JEWISH LIGHTS Publishing.

Charge my credit card: ❏ MasterCard ❏ Visa ❏ Discover ❏ AMEX

Credit Card #_____ Expires _____

Name on card _____

Signature_____ Phone (____) _____

Name _____

Street _____

City / State / Zip _____

SHIP TO / GIFT ORDERS: ❏ Same as Above
Name _____
Street _____
City / State / Zip _____
Gift card to read: _____
_____

Phone or mail to: JEWISH LIGHTS Publishing
Box 237, Sunset Farm Offices, Route 4, Woodstock, Vermont 05091
Tel **(802) 457-4000**   _Fax_ **(802) 457-4004**
Toll free credit card orders **(800) 962-4544** (9AM–5PM EST Monday–Friday)
Generous discounts on quantity orders. Prices subject to change.
Available from better bookstores. Try your bookstore first.
Satisfaction guaranteed